SIMPLIFY CHATGPT

CREATE STREAMS OF INCOME ONLINE, MASTER AI PROMPTS, BOOST PRODUCTIVITY AND GENERATE WEALTH FROM ANYWHERE.

LENA HAYES

CONTENTS

INTRODUCTION

INTRODUCTION

Let me take you back to a time when I was sitting at my kitchen table, staring at my laptop screen like it was a rock brought back from Mars. . A friend of mine had just raved about this new AI tool called ChatGPT. She said it could change my life, save me time, and even open doors to making money online from anywhere.. But there I was,shaking my head like I needed a translator just to understand what ChatGPT was supposed to do. Sound familiar? If you've ever felt a tech-induced panic, you're not alone. And that's exactly why I wrote this book. If you have ever been there, please join me in learning how to use this life changing tool. I am happy you are here to simplify your life with me.

Hello there, I'm Lena Hayes. I have a knack for making complicated tech stuff easy to understand. With a background in digital communication and a love for AI, I've spent years breaking down tech concepts for beginners. As a freelance, faith-filled writer and consultant, I've learned the importance of time-saving strategies and creative solutions in our fast-paced world. I want to share this knowledge with you and help you see technology as a friend, not a foe.

The goal of this book is straightforward: to demystify AI and prompt engineering for beginners. I want to help you overcome your tech fears and discover remote income opportunities. Whether you're new to AI or just looking for ways to work from anywhere, this book is for you.

My primary audience includes beginners to AI and ChatGPT, those hesitant about tech, and anyone seeking remote income opportunities. But if you're an entrepreneur, freelancer, or digital nomad, stick around. There's something here for you too.

Here's the vision in one simple line: I want to give you a clear, actionable approach to using ChatGPT with simplicity. This book will empower you with the skills to embrace AI and explore practical ways to make money from home.

We'll explore key themes like demystifying AI, meaning we will break it down the complex into bite-sized, digestible pieces. We'll dive into AI prompt engineering, showing you how to craft prompts that get the best results. We'll tackle tech fears head-on and provide encouragement through success stories and tips. Finally, we'll delve into remote income opportunities, detailing how ChatGPT can enhance your income possibilities.

Why is this book important now? In today's rapidly changing world, AI tools like ChatGPT are not just buzzwords. They're shaping the way we work and live. As interest in personal and professional growth continues to rise, accepting AI can be a game-changer.

Consider this your call to action. Commit to this journey with me. By the end of the book, you'll have the knowledge and confidence to work with AI effectively. You'll be ready to use it as a transformative tool in your life. You will get better and better at this and your life will change when you apply it..

Here's how the book is structured. We'll start by breaking down AI and ChatGPT, making it as simple as possible. Then, we'll explore prompt engineering and how to craft effective prompts. We'll move on to overcoming tech fears, with relatable examples and success stories. Lastly, we'll dive into remote income opportunities, offering practical ways to make money from anywhere. If you are like me, that is a very appealing benefit to using a device.

As you read, keep this takeaway in mind: You have the potential to transform your life with AI. Whether you want to save time, overcome tech fears, or explore new income avenues, this book will guide you every step of the way.

So, let's get started. Together, we'll turn those tech-induced jitters into confidence and curiosity. Welcome to the exciting world of ChatGPT, where possibilities are endless and within your reach.

1

DEMYSTIFYING AI FOR THE EVERYDAY USER

HAVE you ever had that moment where you're chatting with a friend, and they casually mention "AI," and you're nodding along, pretending to know all about it, while secretly planning to Google it later? You're not alone. AI, or artificial intelligence, often sounds like something out of a sci-fi film, conjuring images of robots taking over the world. But it's not quite that dramatic. AI is more like that super-efficient assistant you've always wanted but couldn't afford. It's here to help make life easier, not complicate it, to simplity it. So let's peel back the layers and see what AI really is, without the intimidating tech jargon.

WHAT IS AI? UNDERSTANDING THE BASICS WITHOUT THE JARGON

At its core, artificial intelligence is about machines doing tasks that typically require human smarts. Think of it as giving computers a kind of "thinking" power, minus the mood swings and caffeine dependency. AI processes information by mimicking human cognitive functions like learning, reasoning, and self-correction. Imagine a student who keeps improving their grades by learning from past mistakes, AI does something similar. It learns from the data it receives, draws conclusions, and corrects itself to get better over time.

Let's talk about learning. In the AI world, learning means absorbing information and turning it into knowledge. For instance, when you teach a computer to recognize cats in photos, it learns by analyzing thousands of cat images. Next comes reasoning and how that works. AI uses logic to solve problems. If you've ever played chess against your phone, you've seen AI reasoning in action. Finally, there's self-correction. AI can fine-tune its processes based on feedback, much like how you might improve your cooking after a few failed attempts at a new recipe.

But AI isn't just for tech nerds or corporations. It's everywhere, subtly making your life more convenient and entertaining. Think about Siri or Alexa—those virtual assistants who can remind you about birthdays or play your favorite song when you're too lazy to get up. They're powered by AI. Or consider Netflix and Amazon, which seem to know exactly what you want to watch or buy next. That's AI at work again, using recommendation systems to analyze your preferences and suggest options you'll likely enjoy.

Now, let's clear up a common misconception: AI isn't trying to replace human intelligence. It lacks the intuition and emotional understanding that come naturally to us humans. While AI can process data faster than we can blink, it doesn't "feel" or grasp the nuances of human emotions. When it comes to creativity and empathy, AI still takes a backseat. A robot might beat you at chess, but don't expect it to write a heartfelt poem or understand why you're crying over a sad movie.

Speaking of which, let's simplify some of that intimidating jargon surrounding AI. Machine learning is one of those terms that get thrown around a lot. Simply put, it's about recognizing patterns in data. It's like teaching a machine to recognize your voice among a crowd by identifying unique patterns in your speech. Then there's neural networks, picture them as systems designed to mimic our brain's structure. Just as our neurons connect to process thoughts and actions, neural networks process data through layers to make decisions. Included with the book are many prompts for you to begin toying with creating your own search engine.

Quick Self-Test: How Many of These Do You Recognize?

Let's see how many everyday AI applications you've encountered. Consider these questions as a fun way to spot AI in your life:

- Have you ever asked Siri or Alexa for the weather forecast?
- Have you noticed Netflix suggesting shows that match your taste?
- Have you shopped on Amazon and seen products recommended just for you?
- Have you used Google Maps for real-time traffic updates?

If you've answered "yes" to any of these, congratulations! You've been interacting with AI without even realizing it.

So, as we kick off this exploration of artificial intelligence, remember that it's not here to intimidate or replace you. It's here to complement your abilities and make your life a bit smoother. As you dive deeper into this book, keep an open mind and embrace the possibilities AI can bring into your life. It's not just about understanding technology, it's about discovering new ways to enhance your day-to-day experiences with tools that are right at your fingertips.

CHATGPT UNVEILED: THE AI THAT'S CHANGING CONVERSATIONS

◆You're having a conversation with your computer, and it feels like you're chatting with a real person. That's the sort of magic ChatGPT brings to the table. Developed by OpenAI, ChatGPT is not just another tech buzzword; it's an AI model that generates human-like text based on the prompts you provide. Think of it as your digital conversation partner, ready to discuss anything from your favorite recipes to the nuances of quantum physics—though it might be more fun to stick with the recipes.

Now, let's get into how ChatGPT actually works its magic. At its core, this AI marvel processes language and crafts responses using sophisticated deep learning techniques. Picture it as a sponge absorbing vast amounts of information from diverse datasets to improve its accuracy. It's like training a dog to fetch by showing it countless examples of successful fetches—except here, we're training an AI to fetch information and respond intelligently.

ChatGPT's conversational prowess is not just for show. Its capabilities extend far beyond casual chit-chat. Businesses use it for customer service automation, making sure you get answers to your queries without waiting on hold for eternity. It's like having a never-sleeping customer service rep at your fingertips. In content creation, ChatGPT lends a hand to writers and marketers, providing a creative boost or even generating entire drafts. Imagine brainstorming with an assistant who never runs out of ideas, always ready to throw another concept your way.

But ChatGPT's power isn't just about what it can do; it's about how easy it makes things for you. Designed with user-friendliness in mind, its interface is as simple as texting a friend. You type in your question or statement, and voila! It responds almost instantly. There's no need for complicated setups or technical expertise. If you can send a text message, you can use ChatGPT. It's that straightforward, and that's what makes it so accessible to everyone, from tech novices to seasoned pros.

Interactive Element: Try This!

Want to see how ChatGPT can assist you? Try this exercise: Think of a topic you're curious about or a problem you need solving. Type it into ChatGPT and see what it suggests. You might be surprised at how quickly it offers insights or solutions.

In the realm of accessibility, ChatGPT is a game-changer. Its straightforward design ensures that everyone, regardless of their tech background, can leverage its capabilities. The interface focuses on ease of use, allowing users to simply input text and receive coherent responses. This simplicity encourages even the most tech-averse individuals to engage with AI without fear or hesitation.

The beauty of ChatGPT lies in its adaptability across various sectors. In customer service, it's automated help desks that respond promptly to inquiries, reducing wait times and improving customer satisfaction. In content creation, writers leverage its ability to generate ideas or even draft articles, enhancing productivity and creativity. It's like having an endless well of inspiration at your disposal, ready to assist whenever you hit a creative block.

For many, the thought of using AI can be daunting. But ChatGPT breaks down those barriers by offering an approachable platform that's easy to navigate. With its simple text input and output, anyone can start using it without needing a degree in computer science. This user-centric focus makes it an ideal tool for exploring the potential of AI in everyday life.

As we explore the capabilities of ChatGPT, it's important to remember that this technology is not just about innovation but also about making life easier. Whether you're using it to automate tasks, generate content, or simply have a chat, ChatGPT is here to enhance your interactions and streamline your processes. So go ahead, give it a try, and discover how this AI marvel can become an integral part of your daily routine, making conversations more engaging and productive than ever before.

And as you experiment with ChatGPT, you'll find that it's not just a tool but a partner in creativity and efficiency.

FROM SCI-FI TO REALITY: AI'S EVOLUTION AND PRACTICAL USES

If you rewind a few decades, artificial intelligence was the stuff of science fiction. Imagine the 1950s, where AI lived in the realm of imagination, with robotic characters gracing TV screens, performing tasks we only dreamed of. fast forward to today, and AI has stepped off the screen and into our daily lives. Ah, the Turing Test—a milestone that marks AI's journey from fantasy to reality. Introduced by Alan Turing in 1950, this test questioned whether a machine could exhibit intelligent behavior indistinguishable from a human. It set the stage for AI's evolution, challenging scientists to create machines that can think—or at least seem to think—like us.

Jumping to the 1970s and 80s, we find expert systems making their debut. These were early forms of AI, designed to mimic human decision-making. Think of them as the great-great-grandparents of today's sophisticated systems. They could solve complex problems in specific domains, like diagnosing diseases or financial forecasting, thanks to their rule-based logic. These systems laid the groundwork for AI's leap from fiction to function.

Today, AI isn't just theory; it's an integral part of our tech-driven lives. Take self-driving cars—once considered a wild idea, now a growing reality on roads worldwide. These vehicles use AI to navigate traffic, recognize road signs, and make split-second decisions that keep passengers safe. Or consider smart home devices that manage everything from lighting to security, learning your habits to optimize comfort and efficiency. It's like having a personal assistant who knows your preferences better than you do.

But what about tomorrow? AI stands on the brink of even more astonishing advancements. In healthcare, personalized medicine is on the horizon, where AI analyzes genetic information to tailor treatments specific to each individual. Imagine a world where your doctor prescribes medication perfectly suited to your unique biology—AI could make that happen. And in education, personalized learning experiences are set to revolutionize how we acquire knowledge. AI can adapt lessons to suit individual learning styles, ensuring every student gets the attention they need. It's education tailored like a custom made suit.

Yet with progress comes responsibility. As AI weaves itself into our lives, ethical questions arise. How do we ensure these powerful tools don't infringe on privacy or perpetuate biases? The deployment of AI must consider its societal impact, balancing innovation with moral responsibility. It's crucial that AI works for humanity, not against it.

The job market is another area feeling AI's influence. Automation is transforming industries, shifting job roles and creating new opportunities while rendering some positions obsolete. While this can be unsettling, it also opens doors for upskilling and new career paths. Emphasizing adaptability ensures that people aren't left behind in this tech-driven era.

Visual Element: Timeline of AI Milestones

There are key milestones like the Turing Test, expert systems, and current innovations into a visual context makes it easier to see AI's journey from concept to integral part of our lives.

As we reflect on AI's path from science fiction fantasy to everyday functionality, we find ourselves at an exciting crossroads. The potential for AI to enhance our world is immense. It promises a future where technology serves as a partner in our daily lives, augmenting our capabilities without overshadowing our humanity. By understanding AI's journey, current innovations, and future possibilities, we equip ourselves with the knowledge needed to grab hold of its benefits while overcoming its challenges intelligently.

COMMON AI MYTHS DEBUNKED: SEPARATING FACT FROM FICTION

When it comes to artificial intelligence, myths abound, and they often overshadow the reality of what AI can actually do. Let's tackle the first big myth: the idea that AI is some kind of omnipotent entity, an all-knowing oracle ready to take over the world. This couldn't be further from the truth. AI, at its core, is a tool designed by humans to perform specific tasks. It's not some all-seeing eye with its own agenda like Big Brother. Even though it feels that way, it doesn't have independent thought. Instead, it's programmed to analyze data and make decisions based on that input. In essence, AI operates within the boundaries set by its creators, relying heavily on human input for direction and purpose.

Next, let's address a common confusion between real AI and the sci-fi portrayals we see in movies. Hollywood loves to dramatize AI as autonomous robots with emotions and desires. But in reality, AI lacks the rich tapestry of human emotions and intuition. While it's great at processing information and recognizing patterns, AI doesn't dream of electric sheep. It can't feel joy or sorrow, nor does it possess creativity in the way humans do. This distinction is crucial because it highlights both AI's power and its limits—it's a sophisticated tool but still just that—a tool. You will figure out how to use the tool, with patience without it belching out foolishness.

Then there's the fear of AI dominance, a narrative that paints a picture of machines rising against their human overlords. While it makes for compelling cinema, in real life, AI's capabilities are tightly bound by human oversight and programming. AI systems rely on humans for maintenance, updates, and direction. They don't self-evolve into smarter or more capable versions on their own. Instead, they are like any software—dependent on continuous human involvement to function effectively and safely. This reliance ensures that AI remains under human control and guidance.

Finally, let's clarify a significant misunderstanding about AI's role in our lives. Many people worry that AI might replace them at work or make humans obsolete in various fields. However, the reality is more collaborative than competitive. AI is designed to enhance human capabilities, not replace them. For instance, in healthcare, AI assists doctors by analyzing medical data to provide insights that aid diagnosis and treatment plans. In business settings, AI tools help analyze market trends and consumer behavior, empowering humans to make informed decisions faster than you ever dreamed possible.

Think about planning a road trip. Traditionally, you'd rely on maps and maybe some friendly advice from fellow travelers. Now, with GPS technology powered by AI, you get real-time updates on traffic conditions and route suggestions tailored to your preferences. The technology doesn't drive the car for you; instead, it augments your decision-making by providing valuable information. That's how AI functions, by making our abilities more productive, rather than taking the wheel entirely.

Myth Buster: Quick Quiz

To put these myths to rest, consider a quick quiz:

1. Can AI feel emotions like a human?
2. Is AI capable of self-improvement without human input?
3. Does AI make humans redundant in their jobs?
4. Is AI capable of creating art with emotional depth?

If you answered "no" to all these questions, you're spot on! These are common misconceptions that often lead to unnecessary fear and misunderstanding.

While it's fun to imagine a world where robots walk among us with feelings and ambitions akin to our own, it's important to ground our understanding in reality. AI is a powerful ally when used wisely. Its true strength lies in its ability to process vast amounts of data quickly and accurately, something our human brains simply aren't built for at such scale.

When we accept AI technology, we open doors to new possibilities—improving efficiency in industries such as finance and manufacturing or revolutionizing our approaches to education and healthcare. But at the heart of every AI application is a human touch—our creativity, intuition, and emotional intelligence remain irreplaceable components of progress.

As we continue exploring the potential of AI throughout this book, remember these truths: AI is not an all-knowing adversary but a powerful assistant capable of enhancing our lives in myriad ways. Recognizing its limitations alongside its capabilities enables us to leverage this technology effectively while dispelling myths that only serve to cloud our judgment and hinder innovation.

AI IN DAILY LIFE: PRACTICAL EXAMPLES YOU CAN RELATE TO

Visualize waking up on a chilly morning, your breath visible in the air. You slide out of bed, and before your feet hit the cold floor, your smart thermostat has already adjusted the temperature, welcoming you into a toasty embrace. That's AI quietly working its magic behind the scenes. These thermostats don't just react; they learn your schedule and preferences, optimizing energy use and keeping you comfortable without you lifting a finger. It's like having a digital butler, ensuring your home is always just right.

Now, picture yourself planning a weekend getaway. You're ready to hit the road, and your navigation app taps into AI to map the best route, avoiding traffic snarls and roadblocks. It's like having a seasoned traveler whispering directions into your ear, ensuring you reach your destination with minimal hassle. By analyzing real-time data, these apps save you time and frustration daily, making travel smoother and more efficient.

But AI doesn't stop there. It's reshaping how we communicate and engage on social media. Remember those eerily accurate content suggestions that pop up as you scroll through your feed? That's AI-powered algorithms at work, curating content tailored just for you. These algorithms analyze your interactions—likes, shares, comments—to serve up posts that resonate with your interests, keeping you engaged longer. It's like having a personal curator who knows exactly what tickles your fancy.

In customer service, AI chatbots are revolutionizing interactions. They're the friendly virtual helpers on websites, ready to assist at any hour. By handling routine inquiries, they free up human agents to tackle more complex issues. These chatbots use natural language processing to understand questions and provide accurate responses. It's like having an eternally patient support rep who never gets tired or cranky. Have you ever gotten made at an chatbot? I have and it doesn't change their answers. It has it's annoying aspects as well, sometimes it is nice to talk to a human.

On the health front, AI plays a crucial role in personal well-being. Imagine a fitness app that doesn't just track your steps but suggests workouts based on your goals and progress. AI-driven apps analyze your activity patterns and offer personalized fitness plans to keep you motivated and on track. It's akin to having a personal trainer in your pocket, constantly encouraging you to push just a little harder.

AI also finds its way into health apps monitoring dietary habits. They track what you eat and provide insights into nutrition, helping you make healthier choices. It's like having a dietician scrutinizing your every meal, minus the judgment. These apps aim to boost your well-being by offering tailored advice that aligns with your health goals.

Shopping has never been more personalized thanks to AI. E-commerce platforms leverage AI to recommend products based on past purchases and browsing history. As you shop online, it's as if there's a savvy salesperson anticipating your needs, suggesting items you didn’t even know you wanted. This personalization enhances the shopping experience, making it more engaging and efficient. The flip side is, we buy things we aren’t even looking to purchase because it is somehow related then pops up to peak our interest.

In entertainment, streaming services use AI to suggest movies and shows tailored to your tastes. By analyzing viewing habits, these platforms curate content that aligns with your preferences. It’s akin to having a film buff friend who always knows what you'd enjoy watching next. This tailored approach ensures you're never at a loss for entertainment options. Amazon uses it to suggest your favorite types of movies. If you are like me, I think, “How does it pretend to know what kind of mood I am in!”

Reflection Section: Think About Your Day

◆ Reflect on how many times AI touches your life daily. Consider the interactions with smart devices or services that simplify tasks or enhance experiences. How does this technology improve convenience or efficiency? What would change if these AI-driven elements vanished overnight? Recognizing AI’s subtle presence highlights its integral role in modern life.

These examples showcase AI's seamless integration into our routines, quietly enhancing convenience and efficiency without fanfare. From adjusting home temperatures to curating personalized entertainment options, AI works tirelessly behind the scenes to make life easier and more enjoyable. As we continue exploring AI's potential, remember that its power lies not in grand gestures but in the small, everyday improvements that collectively transform our experiences.

AI AND YOU: HOW UNDERSTANDING AI CAN TRANSFORM YOUR LIFE

You might feel like you are standing at the crossroads of opportunity and uncertainty. That's where understanding AI can place you, right at the intersection where your personal and professional growth paths expand. Grasping the basics of AI isn't just about keeping up with technology; it's about empowering yourself to enhance every aspect of your life. Whether you're eyeing a career in tech or looking to boost your current role, AI knowledge is your ally. Consider this: tech fields are booming, and the demand for AI literacy is skyrocketing. By embracing AI, you're not just riding a trend—you're future-proofing your career. The more you know about AI, the more you can leverage its power to stand out in a competitive job market. It's like learning a new language that everyone wants to speak.

Diving into the world of AI doesn't have to be scary, you cannot break it. In fact, it can be exhilarating. Picture yourself as a scientist in a lab, experimenting with different concoctions to see what works best. That's the mindset to adopt when exploring AI tools and applications. The market is brimming with apps that cater to various needs—whether it's automating mundane tasks or creating art using algorithms. Why not download a few and see how they fit into your life? Trying out these platforms can spark creativity and offer insights you never imagined possible. It's like having a new toy to play with every day, one that keeps unveiling new tricks.

AI can be your problem-solving partner in crime, especially when it comes to tackling complex issues that require more than just human intuition. Imagine you're knee-deep in data, trying to make sense of endless spreadsheets. AI tools can sift through this information and provide actionable insights, saving you hours of manual labor. They can highlight trends, identify anomalies, and suggest strategies all in seconds. It's like having an extra set of eyes and a brain that never sleeps. This efficiency boost doesn't just save time; it enhances decision-making processes, allowing you to focus on what truly matters.

In today's ever-evolving tech landscape, keeping up with AI trends isn't just advisable; it's vital. Think of it as maintaining a toolbox—each new skill is another tool you can use to build your future. Continuous learning ensures you're not left behind as technology advances. By staying informed about AI developments, you position yourself as an adaptable professional ready to tackle tomorrow's challenges. Whether through online courses, workshops, or even casual reading, expanding your AI knowledge keeps you agile in a tech-driven world.

Let's look at the facts, the world isn't slowing down, and neither should you. As AI continues to shape industries and redefine roles, its influence will only grow. Embracing AI means arming yourself with skills that will keep you relevant. This isn't just about surviving the tech wave—it's about thriving in it. Your ability to learn and adapt will set you apart from those who shy away from change. By understanding AI, you're not just preparing for the future; you're actively creating it.

So, where does this leave us? With an open invitation to explore, experiment, and embrace what AI has to offer. The possibilities are endless, but they start with a single step—understanding. As you continue this journey into the world of AI, remember that knowledge is power. With each concept you grasp and each tool you master, you're not just enhancing your resume—you're transforming your entire life.

In this rapidly changing digital age, AI offers an open door to new opportunities and experiences. Understanding its capabilities can elevate both personal and professional spheres of life, turning challenges into adventures and potential into reality.

2
OVERCOMING TECH FEAR CONFIDENCE AND EASE

FACING YOUR TECH FEARS: A BEGINNER'S GUIDE TO AI

SEE in your mind's eye that you are comfortably sipping your drink at a bustling family gathering when your tech-savvy cousin suddenly whips out the latest in AI technology, a gadget so sleek and innovative it's nearly futuristic. Amidst the excitement, you nod politely, all while secretly harboring the hope that you'll never be required to interact with such complex machines. If this scenario resonates with you, take solace—you're not alone. A multitude of individuals harbor a visceral apprehension towards utilizing AI, haunted by the notion that a mere press of the wrong button could send machines spiraling out of control, echoing dystopian fears of an unintended robot revolution. Realistically, though, these AI tools are calibrated to assist in mundane tasks, from curating the perfect path to a delectable pizza to organizing one's digital calendar, rather than orchestrating grand schemes of world takeover.

Let's undo the tangled brambles of fears that afflict many minds on this technological frontier. Leading the charge is the trepidation of misunderstanding pressing the wrong keys, thus flubbing functionalities. It's not unheard of to dread the unfixable, the irreparable—malfunctions that blur the digital landscape into chaos. Another ominous specter is the fear of data breaches, the ever-present threat lurking in the sprawling digital expanse, preying upon privacy like a silent, pervasive shadow. The notion of one's personal data, laid bare on the ethereal planes of the internet, creates an inherent unrest. Moreover, the foreboding prospect of AI usurping job markets, rendering human skillsets redundant, feeds a fire of insecurity and anxiety of having this technology swiftly eclipse traditional roles.

These fears aren't spontaneous but flourish from roots deeply entrenched in the human psyche. The colossus of change that technological evolution represents can sometimes feel like a treadmill, set at an increasing pace while you frantically search for the off switch just to catch your breath. Historical tech innovations have a storied history of unsettling communities. Take, for instance, times of yesteryear when the advent of trains fueled fears of human bodies succumb to the air pressure of high speeds. AI, similar to these pioneering transformations, stirs similar consternations tied to the uncertain and unfamiliar terrains of advancement.

However, the path forward gleams with opportunity and a beacon of a silver lining. There's solace in knowing these fears can be effectively managed with practical strategies. Start by exposing yourself to AI in manageable doses. Gentle immersion yields comfort—try beginning with simple applications designed to simplify everyday activities, a tentative test of the waters before diving headlong into deeper systems. Engaging in mindfulness practices too, offers a buffer against tech-derived anxieties. Techniques such as focused breathing can clear encumbering clutter in the mind, ushering in a tranquil state from which to calmly engage with technology. (Curb Your Tech Stress with Mindfulness Techniques, 2023).

Let's cultivate an outlook that embraces positive perceptions. Instead of perceiving AI as an antagonist, reframe it as a reliable partner, one that transforms your daily routines into a smoother, more efficient experience. Imagine having a committed digital assistant on call at all hours, optimizing your endeavors and affording you precious moments to savor life. This shift in mindset, from trepidation to curiosity, opens a window to discovery. Regard AI tools as companions in your journey, inserting more ease and enhancements into existence rather than obstructions.

Reflection Exercise: Your AI Comfort Zone

Pause for a moment and think about what elements of AI stir discomfort within you. Is it the intricate complexity of algorithms? The chance for unforeseen errors? Pen these thoughts down, allowing for reflection on incremental steps you can employ to address these reservations. Perhaps it begins by watching an engaging tutorial or experimentally engaging with an AI app that sparks your curiosity. You won't break anything by trying, just jump in!

So, here you stand, at the very intersection where fear clashes with the lure of intrigue. The journey ahead needn't be formidable. Embrace the notion that AI embellishes your skillset rather than supplanting it. With every small stride away from tech-anxieties, you'll cultivate an enriching tapestry of confidence and adeptness. It's about transforming fear into a catalyst for exploration and growth, taking incremental steps towards mastery and empowerment. With time, patience, and openness, the landscape of artificial intelligence will evolve from mountains of apprehension into paths of opportunity.

THE "I'M NOT TECH-SAVVY" MYTH: BUILDING CONFIDENCE IN AI

Ever find yourself muttering, "I'm just not a tech person," as you fumble and wrestle with a new gadget or device? You're not alone. Let's tackle this persistent myth head-on once and for all. You don't need to wield a metaphorical magic wand or be a tech wizard to grasp the nuances of AI. Instead, think of AI as a friendly acquaintance who is merely waiting for you to fully meet and engage with it. Many folks, just like you and me, have started with absolutely zero tech background and now find themselves thriving and coexisting harmoniously alongside AI. Take Susan, for example, who once believed that a "cloud" pertained solely to those beautiful, fluffy formations in the sky. Yet, with growing familiarity and understanding, she now adeptly uses AI to manage her family's small bakery orders, seamlessly balancing her passion for baking with technological efficiency. Or consider Greg, a man who was always more comfortable wielding a hammer rather than navigating a keyboard. Despite his initial apprehension, he now optimizes his construction projects using intuitive AI-driven apps, proving that with a touch of curiosity and a sprinkle of patience, anyone can integrate AI into their life with striking success and sophistication.

The nice thing is that building tech literacy doesn't call for a dramatic lifestyle overhaul, nor does it demand sleep-depriving late-night cramming sessions reminiscent of bygone schooldays. Start small. Begin your journey with user-friendly tutorials, which are abundantly available, designed to guide you step-by-step through the basics without resorting to overwhelming jargon that can often seem arcane. YouTube, along with countless other online platforms, generously offer approachable lessons that demystify complex ideas and turn them into manageable, digestible tasks. Another invaluable option lies in introductory courses. Many of these courses are available for free and are tailored specifically for beginners. They're crafted to walk you through everything from setting up an AI-powered calendar app to mastering ChatGPT for effective brainstorming sessions. Think of it as dipping your toes into gently rippling waters rather than taking an unprecedented plunge into the deep end.

Celebrating small victories is crucial, and that's precisely where small wins come into the picture. Start by setting up a virtual assistant, such as Alexa or Google Assistant, to effortlessly play your favorite tune or remind you of upcoming appointments. It might seem trivial, but it offers a significant confidence boost that should not be underestimated. Next, try organizing your schedule with the aid of an AI-powered calendar app. Once you witness firsthand how these tools can simplify and streamline your life, boosting both efficiency and productivity, your confidence is bound to grow exponentially. You'll likely find yourself pondering how you ever managed to survive and thrive without them.

Community support can be your secret weapon in this ambitious and rewarding tech endeavor. Imagine joining a spirited group where everyone is learning at their own pace, sharing invaluable tips and heartfelt encouragement with each other. Online forums dedicated to AI beginners stand out as excellent starting places. Within these virtual communities, you can freely ask questions without fear of judgment, and bask in the shared triumphs and trials of fellow, enthusiastic learners. Furthermore, local tech meetups and workshops offer another fantastic opportunity for engagement. These events provide face-to-face interactions and hands-on experience, enriching your journey to expertise while boosting your confidence and skill set with every moment spent in these enriching environments.

The journey from "I'm not tech-savvy" to "I can absolutely do this" isn't as daunting or insurmountable as it may initially appear. It's all about changing how you view both technology and yourself. Remember, it's not about becoming a tech guru in a spectacular overnight transformation, but rather about embracing a mindset characterized by gradual learning and ongoing exploration. With each incremental step forward, no matter how minor it may seem in isolation, you are actively building a foundation of confidence that will serve you exceptionally well in this ever-evolving digital age. Just as countless individuals before you have discovered, you, too, can become adept and unflustered by the once-intimidating world of technology.

FROM ANXIETY TO EMPOWERMENT: HOW TO APPROACH AI WITH ENTHUSIASM

Try thinking about it in a different way. You're at a crossroads, paralyzed by the fear of the unknown, staring at the enigmatic AI landscape. But what if that fear could be your compass instead of your roadblock? Consider a different perspective, one where fear fuels curiosity. Instead of dreading AI, let your imagination run wild. What could you achieve if you understood it better? Journaling can be a powerful tool here. Scribble down your thoughts, ideas, and even your worries about AI. As you reflect, watch how your initial apprehension morphs into an eager quest for understanding. It's like turning nervous energy into an enthusiastic sprint towards discovery.

AI isn't some distant, abstract concept. It's already making waves in areas that matter deeply to us. Take healthcare, for instance. AI is aiding doctors in diagnosing diseases quicker and with greater accuracy, potentially saving lives by catching issues early. It offers a second pair of eyes, enhancing the capabilities of medical professionals without overshadowing their humanity. For individuals with disabilities, AI is nothing short of revolutionary. Imagine software that reads text aloud for the visually impaired or apps that translate sign language into speech in real-time. These advancements aren't just tech triumphs; they're life-changing improvements that foster independence and inclusion.

Grasping AI tools can open doors you never imagined. Imagine holding a key that unlocks countless possibilities in both personal and professional realms. Obtaining AI-related certifications could be that key, significantly enhancing your job prospects. Employers are on the hunt for candidates who can navigate the digital landscape with ease and understanding. Knowledge in AI doesn't just make you a more attractive candidate; it positions you as a leader in innovation and problem-solving within your field. It's like having a superpower that others respect and admire, elevating your career trajectory to new heights.

As you make strides in understanding AI, it's important to acknowledge and celebrate these victories, both big and small. Create a milestone tracker for your AI-related goals. Maybe you've successfully automated a task that used to consume hours or developed a basic AI model on your own—these are achievements worth recognizing! Reflect on how far you've come from those first hesitant steps and take pride in the journey of growth you've undertaken. This celebration serves not only as a pat on the back but as motivation for future challenges.

THE ROLE OF AI IN YOUR LIFE: FINDING BALANCE AND HARMONY

We live in an age where every ping or notification can feel like a mini demand on our attention span, which is already stretched thin. So, the trick is finding balance. Incorporate AI into your life in a way that enhances rather than overwhelms. Set clear boundaries, like designated tech-free times to unwind and recalibrate your brain's focus. It's all about using AI to manage your time efficiently without allowing it to monopolize every waking moment. Think of it as having a trusty sidekick: helpful yet unobtrusive.

AI is here to assist, not replace us. Imagine it as an intuitive guide that complements your abilities rather than competing with them. In decision-making, AI offers data-driven insights while still leaving room for human intuition and creativity to shine through. Picture yourself at a crossroads with AI providing clear signposts based on data, but the final choice, whether to turn left or right, is in your hands.

Despite its impressive capabilities, AI can never replicate the warmth of a human smile or the comfort of a friendly chat over coffee. Maintain the human touch in your interactions by prioritizing face-to-face connections whenever possible. Use digital communication as a tool rather than a substitute for real human connection. In a world buzzing with virtual noise, these genuine moments anchor us to what truly matters.

Striking a balance between digital and offline worlds is crucial for maintaining harmony. Establishing routines where you consciously disconnect from technology can provide breathing space for relaxation and reconnection with yourself and others around you. Whether it's reading a book or taking a walk without your phone buzzing in your pocket, these moments of pause allow you to recharge and return with renewed clarity.

Success Stories: How Others Conquered Their Tech Fears

◆ Let's look at some inspiring success stories that breathe life into this narrative of overcoming tech fears with flair and finesse. Meet Alex, a retiree who once viewed technology as an insurmountable challenge but now uses AI to stay connected with family across continents through video calls and virtual reunions. Or consider Sarah, a small business owner who leveraged AI tools to streamline her operations, leading to significant growth in her business—an outcome she never dared dream of before embracing technology.

These stories all share common threads: perseverance amidst doubt, resilience in the face of obstacles, and an unwavering belief in their ability to learn something new. They remind us that mentoring plays an invaluable role on this path, it's guiding hands that help navigate unfamiliar terrain until mastery is achieved.

The Power of Curiosity: Embracing AI as a Learning Journey

Curiosity isn't just about asking questions; it's about embracing learning as an ongoing process filled with wonderment at every turn. Set aside regular time for exploring AI; treat it like an adventure where each discovery leads to more exciting revelations waiting around the corner.

You can take this AI beyond basic applications into creative fields such as art or music where AI continues pushing boundaries in innovative ways, it unveils new dimensions previously unimagined by human minds alone. Personal projects experimenting with AI tools can serve as fertile ground for cultivating fresh ideas while nurturing lifelong learning habits essential for staying ahead amidst rapid technological changes.

As you allow yourself to go deeper into this realm fueled by curiosity-driven exploration, keep abreast of thought leaders shaping its future landscape—gleaning insights from those paving paths toward progress while sharing their passion along each step forward they take together with us all!

THE ROLE OF AI IN YOUR LIFE: FINDING BALANCE AND HARMONY

Incorporating AI into your daily routine can feel a bit like trying to juggle while riding a unicycle, you've got to find that sweet spot where everything works in harmony. The key is balance. Imagine setting digital boundaries like you would set a dinner reservation: firm and necessary. Without them, tech can invade every crevice of your life, causing more stress than relief. Have you ever found yourself scrolling aimlessly through an infinite feed, only to realize you've lost hours? That's tech overload, and it can sneak up faster than you think. Setting limits, like specific hours where the devices take a nap, can protect your mental space. Imagine a tech-free zone in your day, where you simply bask in the analog world. It's liberating, trust me.

AI can be a master of time management, but overreliance might tip the scales away from genuine productivity. It's tempting to let AI handle everything, from reminders to grocery lists, but remember, it's an aid, not a crutch. Think of AI as your sous-chef in the kitchen, helping chop and prep, yet not taking over the entire meal. You still need to taste and adjust the seasoning. Using AI wisely means letting it assist in decision-making without relinquishing control entirely. It's there to support you with data and insights, not to overshadow your human judgment.

Even as AI becomes more part of our lives, maintaining that human touch is crucial. It's easy to get lost in screens and notifications, but nothing beats the warmth of a face-to-face chat. Prioritize these human interactions and gab a coffee with a friend instead of a quick text exchange. You'll find that personal connections foster emotional intelligence in ways AI simply can't replicate. Conversations in person allow for nuance and empathy that no digital medium can fully capture. It's about keeping humanity at the forefront while technology quietly hums in the background.

Balancing the digital and offline worlds can be like walking a tightrope, but with some practice, it becomes second nature. Scheduled tech-free times are your safety net, ensuring you don't tumble into the abyss of constant connectivity. Use this time to reconnect with yourself and others in real life—read a book, take a walk, or simply sit quietly with your thoughts. These moments of pause allow you to recharge and return with renewed clarity and vigor. It's about creating pockets of tranquility amidst the chaos of digital noise.

AI serves as a complement to our abilities without replacing what makes us uniquely human. Consider it as an augmenting force, enhancing our skills and knowledge while leaving room for creativity and intuition to shine. In decision-making processes, AI offers valuable insights that we might overlook but ultimately relies on our discernment to make the final call. It's like having an encyclopedia at your fingertips it is helpful for reference but not a substitute for critical thinking.

In creating this balance, remember that technology should enrich your life, not engulf it. Embrace AI as an ally that streamlines tasks and opens doors to new opportunities without losing sight of the world beyond screens. With thoughtful integration, technology can coexist harmoniously with offline experiences, creating a rich tapestry where both realms complement each other.

As you begin to see this landscape where technology meets everyday life, keep curiosity alive alongside awarenesthese qualities ensure you remain grounded while exploring new frontiers. In each interaction with AI or digital devices, strive for intentionality rather than passivity—be mindful about how these tools impact not only productivity but also well-being.

Using these principles as guideposts helps maintain equilibrium between leveraging technological advancements and nurturing authentic connections within ourselves and with those around us—ultimately leading towards a balanced existence where both digital innovations and analog experiences coalesce seamlessly without detracting from one another's value.

Join this dance between virtual capabilities and tangible realities; savoring each step as you move forward into uncharted territories. Where balance reigns supreme over chaos and where harmony becomes not just attainable but sustainable even in ever-evolving landscapes shaped by innovation's relentless march forward into tomorrow's promise today.

SUCCESS STORIES: HOW OTHERS CONQUERED THEIR TECH FEARS

Let's take a look into the lives of individuals who've faced tech fears head-on—and come out victorious. Take, for instance, Mary, a spirited grandmother in her seventies. She found herself in a tech world she barely understood, yet was determined to stay connected with her grandchildren who lived miles away. With a little nudge from her curiosity and a lot of YouTube tutorials, Mary embraced AI gadgets like smart speakers and video chat platforms. Before long, she was hosting virtual tea parties with her family, complete with laughter and shared stories. Her journey from reluctance to becoming the tech-savvy matriarch of the family reminds us that age is but a number when it comes to embracing technology.

Next, meet Carlos, a small business owner who once viewed AI as an intimidating beast destined to swallow his traditional business practices whole. Yet, he took the plunge into the world of AI applications to streamline his logistics and marketing strategies. By integrating AI-powered customer service bots and data analytics tools, Carlos not only grew his business but also discovered newfound free time to focus on creative projects he truly loved doing.. His tale of transformation speaks volumes about the power of perseverance in leveraging technology for growth. Accepting and integrating the tool makes all the difference.

What can we learn from these stories? Perseverance and resilience stand out as key ingredients for success. Both Mary and Carlos faced initial hurdles and missteps, but they persevered. Instead of giving up at the first sign of trouble, they pushed through the discomfort and emerged more confident for it. Seeking mentorship also played a crucial role in their learning process. Mary reached out to her tech-savvy friend for guidance, while Carlos attended workshops and networked with peers who had successfully integrated AI into their businesses. These mentors provided encouragement and practical advice, helping to demystify unfamiliar territory.

A common theme among these success stories is adaptability. Both individuals embraced change with open minds, willing to learn and unlearn as needed. They understood that continuous learning is vital —technology doesn't stand still, and neither should we. By keeping up with advancements and staying curious, they turned what once seemed daunting into an opportunity for growth and expansion.

As you reflect on these narratives, consider how they might apply to your own experiences. Think about your goals regarding technology. Have you ever thought about what you would like to achieve? Conduct a self-assessment exercise to identify areas where you feel confident and those where you see room for improvement. Perhaps you want to learn how to use AI for personal productivity or explore its applications in your professional life. Whatever your aspirations are, break them down into manageable steps, similar to how Mary tackled video calls one feature at a time. Envision the possibilities that await as you build confidence in using AI tools. It's not about becoming an expert overnight but rather about taking one step at a time towards mastering new skills that enhance your life and those you touch.

Remember that technology isn't an insurmountable mountain but rather a series of hills waiting to be climbed at your own pace. The stories of Mary and Carlos serve as reminders that anyone can overcome tech fears with determination, support, and an openness to learning. So go ahead—take inspiration from their journeys and forge your path towards embracing technology with confidence.

As we continue exploring how others have triumphed over their tech fears, let's keep our curiosity alive and our minds open—because just like Mary and Carlos discovered—there's much more waiting beyond what we initially perceive as barriers or limitations when it comes to engaging with artificial intelligence in meaningful ways!

THE POWER OF CURIOSITY: EMBRACING AI AS A LEARNING JOURNEY

Let's talk about curiosity—that wonderful, insatiable itch to continuously know more, delve further, and truly understand the intricate mechanisms that make things tick. This never-ending quest for knowledge is not merely a hobby; it's a habit, a way of life that breathes vitality into everything you do. When it comes to AI, curiosity stands as your greatest ally, a compass guiding you through uncharted territories. Instead of feeling overwhelmed by the vast expanse and rapid advancements in the domain of AI, think of it as embarking on a thrilling adventure, a journey brimming with endless possibilities and surprises waiting just around the corner.

Consider this exploration of AI like an engrossing hobby that you indulge in with passion and regularity. Dedicate portions of your week to immerse yourself in something new, whether it's soaking in the latest innovation through articles, engrossing yourself in a trail-blazing AI documentary, or diving hands-on into a novel application or tool. The secret lies in making this exploration habitual, not burdensome. Like a gentle river carving valleys over time, consistent curiosity engraves deeper understanding and intimacy with the world of AI. With each piece of knowledge you uncover, the once seemingly intimidating realm of AI transforms into a welcoming companion, laden with potential. As the arc of your understanding extends, the initially daunting landscape of AI will transform to become, with each passing discovery, invitingly familiar and remarkably friendly.

Once the basics have woven themselves into the fabric of your understanding, allow your curiosity to push these boundaries a little further. It is crucial to expand your perspective on AI. It isnot solely a realm of automation and algorithms; it's also a vibrant playground of creativity. Today, forward-thinking artists and pioneering musicians utilize AI in their creative processes, producing artworks that mesmerize with the perfect blend of human imagination and machine precision. Consider dipping your toes into the fascinating world of creative AI projects, imagine generating stunning visuals with AI tools or composing music using sophisticated algorithms. These creative pursuits aren't merely for amusement; they ignite inspiration and ignite innovative ideas, sparking potential breakthroughs in your comprehension and utilization of AI. Who knows? Your next masterpiece, a unique blend of your creativity and an AI program, might be just an experiment away.

Curiosity is often the precursor to innovation and breakthroughs. When you approach AI not as a static subject but with the playful, eager mindset of a child exploring the world, you unlock doors to fresh ideas and novel solutions. Embarking on personal projects serves as a laboratory for experimentation with various AI tools. Perhaps you've been wonderstruck by the potential of AI to assist you in organizing your living space or in managing your finances more effectively. Dive into such intriguing projects with an open-minded approach, allowing the flow of ideas to lead you to possibilities unheard of. Through these explorations, you may unearth innovative solutions that not only simplify your tasks but could potentially inspire those within your community.

You are on a lifelong learning and a curiosity-driven journey with AI mindset. The field of AI is dynamic, continuously evolving, and staying up-to-date necessitates ongoing education and a willingness to learn. Make it a habit to follow thought leaders in the AI space—those inspirational figures who are sculpting the future with their insights, pioneering innovations, and research breakthroughs. Keep an inquisitive eye on emerging trends and developments that could potentially impact your personal and professional landscape. By actively doing so, you're ensuring that your reservoir of knowledge remains fresh, relevant, and poised for application in tangible, real-world scenarios whenever the opportunity arises.

As you nurture this curiosity-centric approach, remember that learning is enriched when shared. It does not have to be a solitary journey through the pages of books or the depths of online articles. Share your intriguing findings and insights with friends or engage in forums and communities where discussions about AI are lively and frequent. Interaction with others can deepen your understanding and offer fresh perspectives that you may not have considered independently.

In wrapping up this chapter, take a moment to appreciate how curiosity has the power to transform reluctance into fascination and obstacles into opportunities. By nurturing and cherishing a sense of wonder with AI, you are empowering yourself to innovate, create, and grow persistently. As you eagerly turn to the next chapter, remember to carry this torch of curiosity along with you. It will serve as your trusted guide as you explore how AI can unlock remote income opportunities, broadening your horizons and widening your potential for remarkable growth.

3
MASTERING AI PROMPT ENGINEERING FOR MAXIMUM EFFICIENCY

THE ART OF PROMPT CRAFTING: GETTING THE BEST FROM CHATGPT

Think about being at a friends dinner party. . The atmosphere is buzzing with excitement, and you're engaged in conversation with someone new, hoping to spark a captivating dialogue that exists beyond the boundaries of small talk. You might start with personal prompts like, "So, what's your story?" or delve into something adventurous with questions like, "Tell me about your last adventure." These are not just questions but carefully crafted prompts, conversational starters that occupy a significant role in guiding the flow and tone of your interaction, steering it toward intrigue, excitement, or laughter. Now, imagine implementing the same methodical approach when interacting with ChatGPT. Just like in human dialogue, prompts expertly guide AI responses and significantly shape the outcome of your exchanges. They're the keystones to unlocking the full potential of AI, setting the stage for responses that can be deeply insightful, wildly creative, or even downright hilarious, depending on how they are shaped and prompted.

Understanding the pivotal role of prompts is crucial for anyone looking to use AI effectively. They act much like a compass, guiding the AI to meticulously navigate through its vast database of knowledge and information. Without clear prompts, you might end up with responses as vague as a cloudy crystal ball reading, an outcome less useful than it could be. Think of them as a meticulously drawn map for your conversation, providing both direction and meaningful purpose. When you define clear objectives for your prompts; whether it's crafting a creative story, solving a problem, or summarizing an academic article simply give ChatGPT a specific target to hit. Clear, well-articulated, and specific prompts are akin to telling a taxi driver your precise destination rather than just saying, "Drive around and let's see where we end up," which might be exciting but not efficient.

Exploring Prompt Variations

Let's delve deeper into experimenting with prompt variations. Just as you might try different conversation starters at that dinner party to see which one garners the best responses, you can easily experiment with how you phrase prompts to ChatGPT. Test them as questions, proposals, commands, or open-ended statements, each carefully tailored for different contexts. Each variation can stimulate a unique type of response from the AI, much like how varying your tone or phrasing in different social scenarios can lead to joyful, insightful, or profound reactions from people. It's essentially about finding what resonates, what triggers the floodgates of creativity or the precision in the AI's reply, much like unlocking a hidden potential.

Learning from AI responses is akin to engaging in a productive two-way feedback loop. When ChatGPT provides you with an answer, pause for a moment to thoroughly analyze it. Why did it work well? What aspects were missing? By dedicating time to reflect on these responses, you refine your prompts and vastly improve future interactions. If a response was spot-on and precisely what you hoped for, consider what elements of your prompt led to that success. If it fell short of expectations, think about how you could rephrase, add more context, or provide more specificity to align the result more closely with your desired outcome next time.

Reflection Exercise: Prompt Perfection

Spend some dedicated time crafting diverse types of prompts for various tasks that interest you. Begin with a simple goal, such as summarizing a complex news article or generating creative ideas for a compelling blog post. Write down three distinct variations of each prompt—possibly one framed as a question, another as a direct command, and a third one as an open-ended invitation. Subsequently, feed these prompts into ChatGPT and meticulously observe the differences in its responses. Take detailed notes on which prompts worked best and theorize why you think they succeeded. This exercise not only sharpens your skills but also helps deepen your understanding of the nuanced complexities involved in prompt crafting, much like a craftsman perfecting their art.

Think of the prompts as the secret sauce in your deep, engaging interactions with ChatGPT. They wield the power to transform mundane exchanges into engaging dialogs filled with potential, insight, and innovation. By mastering the art of crafting effective prompts, you are opening doors to creativity and efficiency that might have seemed locked and unattainable before, leading to richer, more meaningful outputs.

PROMPT ENGINEERING 101: A STEP-BY-STEP GUIDE FOR BEGINNERS

Starting out with prompt engineering is like setting up a treasure map for AI to follow. Each step in crafting your prompt is crucial, starting with defining the desired outcome. Imagine you're standing in a kitchen with all the ingredients for a cake but no recipe. Knowing what you want—whether it's a fluffy sponge or a rich chocolate cake, is your first step. The same goes for prompts. Start by clearly outlining what you want to achieve. Are you looking for a creative story, a quick fact-check, or maybe a detailed summary of a lengthy article? Knowing this helps you set the stage for the AI to deliver relevant and coherent responses. The prompts I have included in your purchase of this book will be a great start.

Once your goal is clear, consider the context and audience, much like choosing the right outfit for an occasion. Context is your backdrop, offering cues that guide the AI's response to fit the setting. Suppose you're writing a prompt for drafting an email. The context could be a formal business inquiry or a casual check-in with an old friend. Each scenario demands different phrasing and tone, and embedding these specifics in your prompt ensures more accurate results from ChatGPT. It's like setting the stage before the big show, ensuring all props are in place for the perfect performance.

Contextual clues can transform a bland prompt into a detailed, engaging one. By embedding background information or specific scenarios, you provide AI with the necessary framework to build its responses on solid ground. For instance, if you're asking ChatGPT to help draft a marketing pitch, including details about the target audience or product features gives it the context needed to generate relevant ideas. Think of these clues as breadcrumbs leading AI through the forest of information to your ideal destination, ensuring it doesn't get lost along the way. It truly is garbage in garbage out scenario.

Incorporating keywords and phrases strategically is sort of like highlighting key passages in a book. They help steer AI towards more targeted outputs by providing signposts along its processing path. Imagine you're prompting AI to generate ideas for social media content; using terms like "engagement," "trending topics," or "audience interaction" can guide its responses towards actionable suggestions. These keywords act as beacons, illuminating the path for AI to follow, ensuring that it remains aligned with your intended direction.

While it's tempting to wax poetic or dive into technical jargon, simplicity and directness often yield better results when crafting prompts. Think of it like giving directions, clear and straightforward language leaves less room for misinterpretation. Avoid complex structures or overly technical terms unless necessary, as they can muddy the waters and lead to ambiguous outputs from AI. Instead, opt for clear instructions that convey your intent without unnecessary embellishments, much like ordering your favorite dish at a restaurant, it's concise but precise.

Understanding common prompting mistakes can save you from future headaches. Ambiguity in prompts is like giving someone directions with vague landmark they will probably get lost. It's not helpful or reliable. When crafting prompts, be specific about what you want AI to achieve. Instead of saying "Tell me about technology," try "Explain how AI is used in education today." This specificity narrows down potential responses and reduces room for error.

Overly complex queries can overwhelm AI like too many cooks in the kitchen spoil the broth. Streamlining prompts by focusing on one idea at a time allows AI to concentrate on delivering accurate results without getting sidetracked by tangential thoughts or concepts. Consider breaking down multifaceted tasks into smaller components that are easier for both you and AI to manage effectively.

Misunderstanding AI's capabilities leads to unrealistic expectations. Your would not expect your cat to perform dog tricks, don't tell Baldazar the cat that. It normally doesn't work that way! Remember that while AI excels at processing information quickly and efficiently, it lacks human intuition and understanding of our unanticipated emotions or abstract concepts. By recognizing these limitations early on, you can tailor your prompts accordingly and avoid disappointments stemming from unfulfilled expectations.

Crafting prompts tailored for real-world applications enhances productivity across various tasks, from email drafting and generating creative content ideas to optimizing workflow efficiency and facilitating learning experiences. For example, using prompts designed specifically for scheduling or task prioritization streamlines routine activities while freeing up time for more meaningful pursuits.

Unlocking creative responses requires advanced strategies that push beyond conventional boundaries, this layers the prompts and adds depth by encouraging detailed exploration of complex topics while experimenting with tone and style generates varied outputs suited for different contexts or audiences.

Interactive exercises offer valuable practice opportunities. You can try creating prompts focused on generating travel itineraries or summarizing complex articles before reviewing AI outputs critically. You could use feedback from these exercises as stepping stones towards refining your techniques further until achieving desired outcomes becomes second nature

As you go deeper into prompt engineering territory remember that continuous practice breeds mastery over time. It can help set personal goals around weekly challenges designed specifically around developing proficiency here; join online forums where shared experiences fuel collective growth among peers similarly invested in honing their craft.

COMMON PROMPTING MISTAKES AND HOW TO AVOID THEM

Let's talk about the elephant in the room, when prompts do stuff you are not wanting from them. Picture this: you're chatting with ChatGPT, and it responds with something that makes you raise an eyebrow. Chances are, the culprit is an ambiguous prompt. Ambiguity sneaks in when language lacks clarity, much like a foggy day obscuring the road ahead. You might ask, "Tell me about technology," and get a response that feels like it was pulled from a random tech encyclopedia, covering everything from typewriters to AI. A prompt like this is sort of like asking someone their favorite movie genre and getting a full history of cinema instead. To avoid this pitfall, specificity is your friend. Instead of casting a wide net, narrow it down. Try, "Explain how AI impacts education today," and watch the magic unfold as ChatGPT delivers more focused insights. It's all about setting clear expectations.

Now, let's tackle overly complex queries. Imagine trying to solve a Rubik's Cube while blindfolded—it's a headache waiting to happen. Overloading prompts with too many ideas or complexities can overwhelm AI, leading to jumbled responses. It's like asking someone to solve world peace and climate change before lunch. Instead, break down your thoughts. Focus on one concept at a time. If you're interested in both AI in healthcare and AI in finance, tackle them separately. This approach not only clarifies your intentions but also prevents overwhelming the AI's virtual brain. Streamlined prompts are your secret weapon, ensuring precise and coherent responses without the clutter.

Then, there's the matter of understanding what AI can and cannot do. Misunderstanding AI's capabilities is like expecting a cat to fetch your slippers. Even Baldazar the cat wouldn't get John's slippers. While AI can process information faster than you can say "supercalifragilisticexpialidocious," it lacks the emotional intelligence and nuance that humans possess. Expecting it to decode sarcasm or understand complex emotional cues as a friend might is setting yourself up for disappointment. Recognizing these limitations helps set realistic expectations and guides you in crafting prompts that align with AI's strengths, like data analysis or generating creative ideas. AI is improving so, your skill set will also as you keep working with it.

Prompt failures aren't the end of the world; they're stepping stones to better interactions. Think of them as the bumps on the road that remind you to slow down and refocus. Every time you send a prompt that misses the mark, take a moment to dissect what went wrong. Was it too vague? Did it ask for something beyond AI's scope? Use these insights to refine your approach. Perhaps you asked ChatGPT to write a poem about "love" and received something that felt off-kilter. By asking for a specific type of love poem, like one about long-distance relationships, you provide clearer guidance for improved outcomes.

Reflecting on these missteps helps hone your skills, transforming mishaps into valuable learning experiences. Consider them as practice rounds in a game where each attempt brings you closer to mastery. With every tweak and adjustment, you become more adept at crafting prompts that yield desired results. It's like learning to ride a bike, remember that wobbles and falls are part of the process before you glide smoothly down the road.

In this journey of prompt refinement, remember that patience and persistence are key. Each interaction with ChatGPT is an opportunity to learn something new about its capabilities and limitations. Embrace the trial-and-error method, viewing each prompt as an experiment in discovery rather than a final exam with only one right answer.

As you continue exploring the world of prompt engineering, keep these common mistakes in mind as guiding stars illuminating your path forward. By recognizing ambiguity, simplifying queries, understanding AI's strengths and weaknesses, and learning from past failures, you're equipping yourself with tools necessary for creating meaningful interactions with ChatGPT.

So go ahead and experiment freely, learn from each iteration, and watch as your skills evolve over time into something truly remarkable!

REAL-WORLD APPLICATIONS: CRAFTING PROMPTS FOR EVERYDAY TASKS

Let's face it, life is full of tasks that could use a little streamlining. Whether it's drafting emails or generating catchy social media content, crafting prompts can make these everyday chores feel like a walk in the park. Imagine sitting down to tackle your inbox and instead of staring at a blank screen, you've got a handy prompt ready to go. Something like, "Draft an email to a colleague about scheduling a meeting next week with a friendly tone." Just like that, you're off and running, and ChatGPT takes your lead, crafting replies that are professional, yet warm. For social media content, think about prompts that spark creativity, like "Generate ideas for Instagram posts promoting eco-friendly lifestyle tips." This nudge can lead to a cascade of fresh ideas, bringing vibrancy and engagement to your digital presence.

Prompts are also fantastic for creative projects, especially when the muse is playing hard to get. Trying to brainstorm novel plots or develop intriguing characters? Use prompts to kickstart the process. Picture this: you're staring at a blank page, waiting for inspiration. Instead of waiting, you prompt ChatGPT with "Suggest a plot twist for a mystery novel set in an abandoned amusement park." Suddenly, you've got ideas flowing like a river in springtime. Characters come to life, stories unfold, and what once seemed like a daunting task becomes an enjoyable exploration of imagination. This approach not only saves time but also enhances creativity by introducing unexpected elements that you might not have considered.

When it comes to improving workflow efficiency, prompts are the secret sauce that transforms chaos into order. Consider using them for scheduling or prioritizing tasks. Imagine waking up and prompting ChatGPT with "Plan my day with top priorities including work meetings and personal errands." In seconds, you've got a structured plan that helps you tackle your to-do list with ease. Prompts can turn routine chaos into seamless productivity, ensuring nothing slips through the cracks while optimizing your time management skills. They're like having an efficient assistant who doesn't demand coffee breaks or complain about Mondays.

Prompts can also be your best friend in learning and research. If you're knee-deep in educational pursuits or information gathering, they can guide you through the process like a seasoned tour guide. Let's say you're researching climate change impacts; a prompt like "Summarize recent studies on the effects of climate change on polar bear populations" can quickly provide a concise overview without sifting through mountains of data. This approach not only saves time but also enhances comprehension by distilling complex information into digestible insights. It's like having a personal research assistant who's always ready to help summarize articles or formulate questions for deeper exploration.

Interactive Element: Craft Your Own Prompt

Here's a fun exercise: Think of an everyday task you'd like to simplify. Maybe it's meal planning, organizing your workspace, or even planning a weekend getaway. Write down three different prompts that could help streamline this task. For instance, if it's meal planning, try prompts like "Provide a weekly meal plan for a family of four focusing on healthy recipes," "Suggest grocery lists based on this meal plan," or "Create dinner ideas for busy weeknights using pantry staples." Experiment with phrasing to see what generates the most helpful responses. This exercise not only hones your prompt crafting skills but also demonstrates how versatile and impactful prompts can be in optimizing daily routines.

Crafting prompts tailored for real-world applications isn't just about enhancing productivity—it's about transforming how you approach everyday challenges. By integrating prompt engineering into your daily routine, you unlock new levels of efficiency and creativity.

Whether it's drafting emails, generating content ideas, streamlining workflows, or facilitating learning, prompts empower you to navigate tasks with ease and confidence. They're the bridge between intention and action, offering clarity and direction in an often chaotic world.

With practice and experimentation, you'll find that prompts become second nature—an intuitive tool that enhances every aspect of your life. So go ahead and explore the possibilities; discover how prompt engineering can elevate your daily experiences from mundane to extraordinary.

ADVANCED PROMPT STRATEGIES: UNLOCKING CREATIVE RESPONSES

Have you ever walked into an art studio? When surrounded by canvases, you look around searching for a splash of color and imagination. Crafting advanced prompts is quite similar; it's about layering ideas to create a masterpiece. Think of multi-layered prompts as building a sandwich, where each layer adds depth and flavor to your AI interaction. Start with a base prompt—something straightforward, like asking ChatGPT to draft a story introduction. Then, add layers with follow-up prompts to dive deeper into character development or plot twists. It's like adding your favorite toppings, each contributing to the final taste. These layers invite ChatGPT to weave more detailed and complex responses, offering richer narratives that unfold like the chapters of an engaging novel.

Ever tried on different outfits to see which one fits the mood? Playing with tone and style in your prompts is somewhat like that fashion experiment. You can request ChatGPT to respond in varying tones, from formal to downright goofy, depending on the task at hand. Imagine asking for a formal business proposal one moment and a humorous skit about penguins the next. It's like having a chameleon conversation partner, ready to adapt and entertain. You might say,

"Write a job application in a professional tone," and then switch it up with, "Now, tell me a joke in the style of a stand-up comedian." This flexibility opens doors to creative content that fits any scenario, whether it's serious or light-hearted.

Creating narratives or developing ideas step-by-step through prompt sequencing is similar to assembling a jigsaw puzzle. Each piece connects to the next, gradually revealing the bigger picture. Start with an initial scene or idea, then guide ChatGPT through subsequent prompts to build story arcs or elaborate on concepts incrementally. It's like setting up dominos; the thrill lies in watching each piece fall perfectly into place, creating an intricate storyline. By structuring your prompts in sequence, you can guide ChatGPT from introducing characters to unraveling climaxes, crafting cohesive and compelling narratives that captivate readers.

Exploring unconventional prompt types can yield unique outputs that surprise and delight. Imagine stepping outside the box and using visual or sensory-based prompts to stimulate ChatGPT's responses. It's like painting with words, where you describe a scene not just through action but through sensory details—sights, sounds, smells. Consider a prompt like, "Describe the smell of freshly baked bread in a bustling Parisian bakery." This approach encourages ChatGPT to tap into its descriptive abilities, producing responses rich with imagery and emotion. Such prompts transform interactions into immersive experiences, where AI conjures vivid scenes that resonate on deeper levels.

Visual Element: Prompt Reflection

Grab a notebook and pen, then jot down an array of creative prompts you'd like to experiment with. Start with simple ideas—perhaps a humorous take on a historical event or a sensory description of your favorite place—and build layers by considering different tones or styles. Reflect on how these variations might affect the responses you receive from ChatGPT. This exercise not only nurtures your prompt crafting abilities but also offers insight into how nuanced adjustments can lead to unexpected and delightful outputs.

Advanced prompt strategies are like unlocking a treasure trove of creativity, offering endless possibilities for engaging interactions with ChatGPT. These techniques not only enhance your ability to communicate effectively with AI but also inspire innovative thinking across various domains. Embrace the challenge of crafting layered prompts, experimenting with tones, sequencing narratives, and exploring unconventional formats—you'll discover new dimensions in your AI interactions that enrich both personal projects and professional endeavors.

Interactive Exercises: Practice Your Prompt Crafting Skills

Have you ever dreamed of an exhilarating and unforgettable getaway? You have the entire world at your fingertips, and the possibilities before you seem utterly infinite. The thought of orchestrating such an adventure might appear overwhelming when faced with a myriad of details. But why not let the powerful capabilities of AI take on some of that burden? Dive into this exercise by crafting an insightful yet simple prompt like, "Create a travel itinerary for a week-long adventure in Greece, focusing on historical sites and local cuisine." Engage with ChatGPT to see how it might deftly sculpt a detailed plan that could include everything from meandering through the ancient and storied streets of Athens, absorbing the historic ambiance, to savoring exquisite moussaka by the serene and beautiful Aegean Sea under the warm, golden sun. This exercise serves a dual purpose: it not only helps you hone your prompt crafting skills but also provides a tantalizing glimpse into how AI can transform intricate planning from a mundane chore into an adventurous journey filled with unexpected possibilities.

Now, switch gears into something decidedly more cerebral and intellectually stimulating. Choose an intricate article—imagine one detailing AI's significant impact on climate change—and formulate a capable prompt designed to summarize it with clarity and conciseness. Perhaps you use, "Summarize the key points of this article on AI's role in climate change mitigation." As ChatGPT diligently works through your request, take note of its ability to distill dense and often complex information into succinct, understandable insights. These exercises serve as your evolving playground, offering you hands-on practice in crafting prompts that are strategically targeted and effective, enhancing both your skill and confidence.

Feedback can become your greatest ally in perfecting your prompt techniques. Each time you run your prompts through ChatGPT, make a comparison of the responses you receive from different variations. Did one specific prompt yield a vibrant and more detailed itinerary compared to another? Did a subtle adjustment remarkably enhance the clarity or impact of your article summary? Engaging in this reflective process enables you to pinpoint and appreciate what works and what might not, allowing you to fine-tune your approach with each engaging attempt. It's very much like having an introspective conversation with a thoughtful mentor who offers gentle guidance and encouragement, nudging you toward improvement with every insightful piece of feedback.

But don't hoard these newly discovered skills for yourself—collaboration can be an enormously rewarding enterprise. Consider joining online forums, discussion boards, or writing groups where you can share your prompts, experiences, and gathered insights with others. Exchanging ideas and learning from fellow enthusiasts not only enriches your personal understanding but also exposes you to fresh and diverse perspectives. Imagine it as joining a vibrant book club, but one dedicated to the art of prompt crafting, where each participant contributes their unique observations and experiences, ultimately enhancing the collective knowledge and skill set of the group.

Regular practice remains essential to master any skill, and prompt engineering is by no means an exception to this rule. Set personal goals for yourself, such as weekly prompt challenges that push your creative boundaries and foster continuous growth. Perhaps you even commit to crafting five novel prompts each week, exploring different styles and tones along the way. Over time, these small but deliberate efforts accumulate, steadily building a robust foundation of expertise and competence that empowers you to tackle any task with both confidence and creativity.

As we bring this chapter to a close, remember that the journey to mastering prompt engineering is one richly filled with exploration, creativity, and collaboration. It involves embracing the iterative process of learning, growing from each success as well as every setback, and consistently seeking fresh opportunities for development. Each prompt you craft inches you closer to unlocking the vast potential of AI as a versatile tool for innovation and efficiency. In our next chapter, we will delve into how AI has the potential to open new doors to remote income opportunities, turning your refined skills into a source of financial empowerment and independence.

"The best way to find yourself is to lose yourself in the service of others."

— MAHATMA GANDHI

People who give without expecting anything in return live happier lives. So, let's make a difference together!

Would you help someone just like you—curious about ChatGPT but unsure where to start?

My mission is to make ChatGPT for everyone.

But to reach more people, I need your help.

Most people choose books based on reviews. So, I'm asking you to help a fellow Tech Nerd by leaving a review.

It costs nothing and takes less than a minute but could change someone's journey. Your review could help...

...one more small businesses provide for their community.
...one more entrepreneur support their family.
...one more employee get meaningful work.
..one more client transform their life.
...one more dream come true.

To make a difference, simply scan the QR code below and leave a review:

If you love helping others, you're my kind of person. Thank you from the bottom of my heart!

Lena Hayes

4
INTEGRATING AI INTO YOUR DAILY ROUTINE

AI AS YOUR PERSONAL ASSISTANT: STREAMLINING DAILY TASKS

Imagine waking up to the aroma of freshly brewed coffee while the world outside is still rubbing the sleep from its eyes. Your smart assistant already sorted your emails, prioritized your schedule, and even reminded you to pick up milk on the way home. Sounds dreamy, right? AI has become a digital genie, ready to grant your productivity wishes with just a few commands.

First, let's tackle those pesky repetitive tasks that gnaw away at your precious time like a hungry squirrel on a nut binge. AI's capable of automating these, giving you more time for things that tickle your fancy. Consider email filtering. AI algorithms act like a diligent secretary, sorting through the chaos of your inbox, prioritizing important messages, and even gently nudging spam into the trash. No more drowning in a sea of unread emails. Furthermore, social media has a knack for consuming time without warning. With AI scheduling, posts can be planned and automated days or even weeks ahead, freeing you to focus on creating engaging content instead of scrolling endlessly.

Have you ever stared at your calendar, baffled by overlapping appointments and meetings that seem to multiply overnight? AI-powered calendar apps are here to rescue you from scheduling chaos. They analyze your availability and suggest optimal meeting times, ensuring no more awkward double-booking situations. Imagine telling Siri or Alexa to set a reminder for tomorrow's presentation at work or your evening yoga class. These voice-activated reminders make sure you're always on top of your game, without the hassle of manually setting alarms for every task.

When it comes to managing tasks, AI is like that friend who knows you better than you know yourself. It learns your preferences and adapts to your habits over time. Ever thought about having a digital assistant that suggests tasks based on your daily routine? AI apps can do just that, optimizing how you manage tasks by updating customizable to-do lists as you complete each item. It's like having a personal planner adjusting itself in real-time to suit your life's rhythm.

Virtual assistants have revolutionized how we manage our lives, seamlessly integrating into our daily routines. Imagine having all your tasks centralized in one place, organized neatly by your trusty assistant. Using Alexa or Google Assistant, you can voice-activate updates for task lists, control smart home devices, and even ask it to read out your schedule for the day—all without lifting a finger. It's like having a personal butler who doesn't need coffee breaks.

Interactive Element: Task Automation Checklist

Create a checklist of daily tasks you'd like to automate using AI. Start small: think email sorting, social media posts, and setting reminders. Identify which virtual assistant or AI tool suits each task best. As you experiment with these tools, note improvements in efficiency and time saved. Reflect on how these changes impact your productivity and well-being.

Now that you've got a peek into how AI can streamline your day-to-day life, imagine the possibilities as these technologies continue to evolve. We're living in an age where digital tools are not just helpful but transformative. Whether you're managing a household or steering a business ship through turbulent waters, AI is there as a steadfast ally. Embrace it, and watch as those mundane tasks melt away like snow in springtime, revealing more room for creativity and joy in your daily endeavors.

TIME MANAGEMENT WITH AI: CREATING MORE HOURS IN YOUR DAY

Have you ever had a day so organized it feels like you've added a couple of extra hours to the clock? That's because AI stepped in, waving its magic wand. Start with prioritizing tasks. AI tools are like those smart planners that adjust priorities based on deadlines. You tell them what's urgent, and they sort everything out, making sure you're not scrambling at the last minute. Picture a day where you tackle the big stuff first, leaving the rest to fall into place like a perfectly arranged puzzle.

Now, let's talk about time analysis. Ever get to the end of a day and wonder where all those hours went? AI tools can help track how you spend your time, highlighting inefficiencies like a spotlight in a dark room. These apps show you how much time you spend on email, social media, or even just staring blankly into space. They generate reports that expose those sneaky time-wasting activities, offering insights that make it easier to tweak your routine for maximum efficiency.

Streamlining workflows is another AI superpower. Consider workflow automation software that takes care of routine business processes, reducing the time you spend on mundane tasks. AI-driven project management tools enhance team collaboration, ensuring everyone is on the same page without endless meetings. They're like the conductor of an orchestra, guiding each section to create a harmonious symphony of productivity.

Decision fatigue is real, and AI can lighten that mental load with quick, data-driven recommendations. Imagine an AI algorithm suggesting your daily outfit based on weather predictions—no more staring at your closet in despair. It's like having a personal stylist who knows exactly what will keep you comfy and chic. These recommendations save time and mental energy, allowing you to focus on decisions that truly matter.

AI's role in time management is not just about efficiency but also about creating balance. By optimizing how you allocate your hours, AI helps you find time for the things you love, whether it's spending more moments with family or pursuing that hobby you've always wanted to try. It's about living a life where work doesn't overshadow everything else.

As your digital ally, AI empowers you to reclaim your day, transforming how you manage tasks and time. These tools are not just gadgets but partners in productivity, helping you navigate the chaos with ease and clarity. It's about finding harmony in the hustle and bustle, allowing more room for joy and creativity.

Deciding to make AI part of your routine can feel like having a team of experts at your disposal, ready to assist with everything from scheduling to decision-making. These innovations offer a glimpse into a future where technology supports rather than overwhelms. They're here to guide you through the maze of modern life with confidence and ease.

Realizing the potential of AI in personal productivity is not just about keeping up with trends but about enhancing your quality of life. It's about stepping into a space where technology simplifies rather than complicates—where it serves as an extension of yourself rather than an obstacle.

With AI by your side, each day becomes an opportunity to explore new ways of being productive without sacrificing well-being. It's about embracing change with open arms, welcoming technology as a friend rather than fearing it as a foe.

Think of AI as that reliable friend who always has your back, ready to lend a hand whenever needed. Whether organizing tasks or providing timely recommendations, these tools make everyday life smoother and more manageable.

Embrace these advancements not just as innovations but as enhancements to how we live and work. They're here not only to streamline processes but also to enrich experiences, making time management less about ticking boxes and more about achieving fulfillment.

With AI's support, every day is a chance for growth without stress—a journey towards becoming more efficient while remaining true to yourself. Let these tools guide you towards greater productivity without losing sight of what truly matters—finding joy in both the little things and grand adventures alike.

ENHANCING PERSONAL PRODUCTIVITY: AI TOOLS AND TECHNIQUES

Picture yourself in a local coffee shop,, laptop open, ready to take on the day. The aroma of coffee fills the air, and a soft hum of chatter surrounds you. As you dive into work, AI tools become your silent partner, minimizing distractions and enhancing focus. Apps like Freedom or Cold Turkey block distracting websites during work hours, preventing endless scrolling through social media rabbit holes. It's like having a digital bouncer, keeping unwanted interruptions at bay. With these tools, you're free to immerse yourself in deep work, knowing that your attention won't be hijacked by the latest viral cat video.

Creativity sometimes needs a nudge, and AI can be that gentle tap on the shoulder. Consider AI tools designed for brainstorming and mind mapping. Think of them as your digital muse, offering fresh perspectives and helping you weave ideas into a cohesive tapestry. Whether you're sketching out a new business plan or crafting a novel, these tools provide the spark that ignites your creative flame. And when writer's block strikes, creative writing assistants can suggest plot twists or character development paths, turning a daunting blank page into a canvas for storytelling. It's like having a co-author who never gets tired or runs out of ideas.

Learning new skills or enhancing existing ones has never been more accessible with AI-powered resources. Imagine language learning apps tailored to your personal pace, offering lessons that adapt based on your progress. It's like having a personal tutor in your pocket, ready to guide you through conjugations and vocabulary drills at any moment. For those diving into the world of coding, AI-driven platforms offer exercises with real-time feedback, transforming learning into an interactive experience. These resources ensure that no matter where you are on your learning journey, there's always room for growth and improvement.

Customization is key when it comes to productivity tools, and AI is adept at tailoring solutions to fit individual needs. Picture configurable dashboards that display the metrics most relevant to you. Whether it's tracking project deadlines, monitoring fitness goals, or keeping an eye on your budget, these dashboards offer a personalized snapshot of your priorities. By providing a clear overview of tasks and progress, they empower you to manage your time and resources effectively. It's akin to having a command center at your fingertips, where you can swiftly navigate the demands of daily life.

In this digital age, AI serves as both a guide and a companion in our quest for productivity and creativity. These tools not only enhance efficiency but also enrich our experiences, making every day an opportunity for exploration and achievement. Imagine waking up each morning with a sense of excitement for what lies ahead, knowing that AI is there to support you every step of the way. Whether it's blocking distractions, sparking creativity, facilitating learning, or customizing productivity tools, AI transforms the way we live and work.

As we begin to accept all these advancements, we find ourselves more capable and confident in navigating the complexities of modern life. With AI by our side, we have the freedom to focus on what truly matters—whether it's pursuing our passions, building meaningful connections, or simply enjoying moments of tranquility amidst the hustle. In this ever-evolving landscape, AI stands as a testament to human ingenuity and its potential to enhance every facet of our existence.

THE SMART HOME: USING AI TO SIMPLIFY HOUSEHOLD MANAGEMENT

Imagine walking into your home and everything just works. The lights dim to match the setting sun, the thermostat adjusts to your ideal cozy temperature, and you didn't have to lift a finger. This isn't some far-fetched sci-fi dream—it's the magic of AI in the smart home, taking on tasks we never thought possible. Smart thermostats, for instance, are like having a personal climate concierge. They learn when you're home, when you're out, and adjust temperatures accordingly. No more fiddling with dials or waking up in the middle of the night to a freezing house. They help save energy by ensuring your heating or cooling systems are only working when needed, which is a win for both your wallet and the planet.

Then there's AI-powered lighting, acting as an intuitive lighting designer in your home. These systems can respond to natural light levels, adjusting brightness throughout the day to match the ambience outside. Imagine reading in the living room where the light gently brightens as clouds pass over, or dims in sync with the setting sun during a cozy evening. It's all about creating harmony between your indoor space and the world outside, seamlessly integrating nature into your living environment.

Security is another area where AI shines, transforming our homes into safe havens. AI surveillance systems don't just record footage; they learn and recognize familiar faces, alerting you to unfamiliar visitors. Picture this: You're on vacation and get a notification on your phone because someone's at your door. It's just the neighbor dropping by to water your plants, and you can relax knowing your home is safe. Smart locks add another layer of security, letting you control access from anywhere. Whether it's unlocking the door for a friend or making sure you didn't forget to lock up on your way out, these features offer peace of mind wrapped in convenience.

Chores might be the bane of many people's existence, but AI is here to change that narrative too. Robotic vacuum cleaners zoom around your home like diligent little helpers, navigating furniture and dodging obstacles with ease. They work while you're out, ensuring you return to a clean floor without lifting a broom. In the kitchen, smart appliances suggest recipes based on what's already in your pantry. Imagine opening your fridge, unsure of what to make for dinner, and your oven suggests a delicious meal using those random ingredients you've been ignoring. It's like having a personal chef who knows exactly what's available and how to make it work.

The synergy between AI and IoT devices is where things get truly exciting. It's like having a symphony conductor for your home, ensuring every device works in harmony. A centralized control hub allows you to manage all your smart devices with ease. Want to dim the lights, lock the doors, and start a playlist? You can do it all with a simple voice command or tap on your smartphone from anywhere in the house, or even from halfway across the world if you're traveling.

In this interconnected ecosystem, everything is tailored to fit your lifestyle. Your home becomes a dynamic space that adapts to your needs rather than demanding constant manual adjustments and attention. It's about creating an environment that feels both futuristic and comfortably familiar, where technology enhances rather than complicates daily life.

Home automation is not just about gadgets; it's about reclaiming time and adding layers of comfort and safety to our lives. Whether it's ensuring energy efficiency or making sure you're not left in the dark—literally or figuratively—AI transforms our homes into spaces that work as hard as we do.

AI IN PERSONAL FINANCES: BUDGETING AND FINANCIAL PLANNING

Picture yourself sitting at a café, sipping a latte, and your phone vibrates with an alert. It's not a text from a friend but a gentle nudge from your AI finance app, reminding you that you're about to deviate from your monthly budget. How cool is that? With AI-driven budgeting, keeping track of your expenses becomes as easy as ordering another coffee. These clever apps categorize your spending, showing you exactly where your money goes. They act like digital accountants, analyzing spending patterns without charging you an arm and a leg. Automated alerts swoop in when you're about to splurge too much on those irresistible online shopping sprees.

Now, let's switch gears to investments. Imagine having a financial advisor who's never been late to a meeting and doesn't charge hourly rates. Enter robo-advisors, the unsung heroes of smart investment tools. They tailor investment strategies based on your individual goals, whether it's saving for that dream vacation or building a nest egg for retirement. These savvy algorithms analyze market trends and rebalance your portfolio, ensuring you're putting your money where it matters most. It's like having a wise old uncle who knows his stocks from his bonds, but with none of the unsolicited advice at family dinners.

Ever felt lost in the maze of personal finance? AI-driven platforms offer interactive courses to boost your financial literacy. Picture this: you're navigating through an engaging module on compound interest, and it finally clicks! These resources take complex financial concepts and break them down into bite-sized lessons. They're like having a patient teacher who doesn't mind repeating the lesson until you get it. Armed with this knowledge, you can make informed decisions about credit scores, mortgages, or even deciphering your paycheck deductions.

Let's not forget about security which is such an essential component of managing finances. AI steps up its game with fraud detection and prevention. Think of algorithms acting like vigilant watchdogs over your transactions. They sniff out unusual activity quicker than you can say "identity theft," alerting you to potential threats. It's like having a security detail for your bank account, ensuring peace of mind even when you're enjoying that beach-side vacation. These vigilant systems keep your finances safe from prying eyes and sticky fingers.

In this digital age, managing personal finances no longer feels like navigating a labyrinth blindfolded. With AI at your side, budgeting and expense tracking are streamlined, leaving you more time to focus on what truly matters—like planning that next adventure or enjoying a guilt-free shopping spree. As you sip your coffee, knowing your finances are under control, it's clear that AI isn't just about tech wizardry; it's about empowerment and making life simpler.

The beauty of these technological advancements lies in their ability to adapt to individual needs. Whether you're just starting on the path to financial independence or looking to optimize existing strategies, AI tools offer tailored solutions for everyone. These tools provide the flexibility needed to accommodate varying lifestyles and preferences while maintaining efficiency and accuracy.

The integration of AI into personal finance management has revolutionized how we approach budgeting and investment planning. What once required hours of manual tracking and analysis can now be accomplished with minimal effort thanks to intelligent algorithms that do the heavy lifting for us.

With enhanced security measures in place, there's less worry about potential threats lurking in cyberspace. The combination of automated alerts and advanced detection algorithms ensures that any suspicious activity is promptly addressed before it escalates into a significant issue.

Incorporating AI into financial planning is not just about convenience; it's about creating opportunities for growth and empowerment. By leveraging these tools effectively, individuals can take charge of their financial futures with confidence knowing they have reliable support at their fingertips.

As technology continues its rapid evolution, the possibilities for personal finance management seem endless. From budgeting to investments and beyond, AI offers unprecedented access to resources that empower individuals to achieve their goals more efficiently than ever before.

By embracing these innovations wholeheartedly, we open doors previously thought inaccessible, transforming the way we manage our finances while enjoying newfound freedom in both time and resources!

HEALTH AND WELLNESS: HOW AI CAN SUPPORT YOUR WELL-BEING

Imagine a world where your health and wellness have a digital ally, diligently attentive and ever-ready to assist you in a seamless and efficient manner. AI has made that possible, revolutionizing how we perceive and pursue our wellness goals, transforming them from distant dreams into achievable realities.

AI-Powered Health Monitoring

First up, let us step into AI-powered health monitoring, a realm where advanced technology intertwines with daily life, acting much like your personal health detective. These sophisticated tools are consistently on the lookout, seamlessly tracking your vital signs through wearable devices and digital applications. Whether it's your heart rate, sleep patterns, or activity levels, these ingenious gadgets maintain a vigilant eye, poised to flag any anomalies. Picture yourself adorning a sleek, unobtrusive wristband that meticulously collects data, discreetly alerting you if your heart rate spikes while engrossed in a suspenseful movie or overexerts during an intense workout. It's sort of like to having a miniature doctor on your wrist, ensuring that you're perpetually in tune with your health status, empowering you to make informed decisions that foster your well-being.

Personalized Fitness Programs

Let's pivot to the concept of personalized fitness programs where AI emerges as your ultimate fitness confidant. Imagine an AI application that becomes an intrinsic part of your fitness journey, synthesizing data to curate workouts that are as unique as you are. Have a cherished goal to run a marathon, or perhaps a simple wish to fit back into those beloved jeans from last summer? These intuitive apps meticulously tailor workouts, aligning them intricately with your personal pace, responding astutely to your feedback and progress. As exercise evolves from being a mundane task into an exhilarating journey, it adapts richly to your accomplishments and challenges, providing encouragement during plateaus and celebrating when you break new ground. This is motivation in its most advanced, user-friendly form—a fusion of technology and personal empowerment that propels you towards healthier living, without the daunting presence of crowded gyms full of strangers or the intimidating gaze of others.

AI-Supported Mental Health

Mental health occupies an equally significant pedestal alongside physical health, and AI is stepping boldly into the limelight to offer invaluable support. Envision engaging in a comforting dialogue with an AI chatbot that listens intently, without judgment, while offering exercises designed to fortify your mental resilience. These digital companions provide a bucolic refuge—a safe place where you can freely vent, introspect, or indulge in mindfulness techniques. It's similar to carrying a therapist in your pocket, available on-demand without the pressure of fixed appointments or time constraints. Whether grappling with everyday stressors or seeking moments of tranquility in a bustling day, these resources stand by, offering solace, strategies, and a roadmap to mental fortitude.

Navigating Nutrition with AI

Nutrition, often overshadowed by a loud clashing of conflicting advice and myths, finds clarity through AI's unwavering guidance. Equipped with insightful apps that craft meal plans meticulously tailored to your specific dietary preferences and nutritional needs, discerning what's healthy becomes refreshingly easy. Imagine an app cognizant of your decision to cut back on sugar, skillfully suggesting dinner recipes that are not only satisfying but also congruent with your dietary goals. It's like having a seasoned culinary expert at your side, navigating you through the sometimes overwhelming landscape of dietary choices, ensuring every bite is both delectable and nutritious.

Embracing AI for Enhanced Wellness

As we continue to integrate AI into our daily wellness routines, the potential to enhance our quality of life becomes increasingly apparent. With the aid of continuous health monitoring, personalized fitness regimens, mental health support, and nutrition management, AI metamorphoses wellness aspirations into attainable realities. It's about living your life with an enhanced layer of support where technology serves to amplify your concerted efforts rather than convolute or obstruct them.

In wrapping up this segment, it is crucial to remember that AI in this context goes far beyond mere algorithms and data processing. It embodies the creation of a supportive, nurturing environment conducive to personal growth and enhanced well-being. As we embrace these advanced tools, we unlock opportunities for healthier, more autonomous lifestyles, free from the stress of navigating complexity alone. The ensuing chapter will take us deeper, delving into how AI can fundamentally revolutionize learning and creativity —transforming potential into tangible achievements and dreams into living realities.

5
EXPLORING REMOTE INCOME OPPORTUNITIES WITH CHATGPT

FREELANCING WITH AI: OPPORTUNITIES IN CONTENT CREATION AND BEYOND

Picture this: You're lounging at your favorite café, laptop open, latte in hand, and the soft jazz playing in the background. You've just landed a freelance gig, and you're ready to dive into the world of content creation. But instead of staring at a blinking cursor, waiting for inspiration to strike, you have ChatGPT as your trusty companion. With this AI tool, generating high-quality content becomes less about waiting for the muse and more about crafting precise prompts that guide the AI to produce exactly what you need. 💰

Writing blog posts and articles no longer feels like a daunting task. You start by brainstorming with ChatGPT, throwing around ideas like you're playing catch with a friend. It's like having a brainstorming buddy who's always ready to toss back ideas, refined and polished, just waiting for your unique touch. Need SEO-optimized content? ChatGPT's got your back. It can suggest keywords and structure your content to attract those elusive search engine spiders, helping your work rise through the ranks in no time.

But let's not stop at writing. Freelancing with AI isn't just about churning out words; it's about enhancing every creative project you take on. Imagine crafting engaging social media posts with AI suggestions that capture the essence of what you want to convey. These posts are not only eye-catching but also tailored to resonate with your audience, making them stop mid-scroll for a second glance. Or perhaps you're developing scripts for video content. ChatGPT can help outline scenes and dialogue, ensuring your message stays clear and captivating from start to finish.

Communication is key in freelancing, and AI tools can streamline client interactions, making you look like the organized professional you are. Automated email responses for client inquiries ensure no message goes unanswered. Imagine setting up an AI assistant that filters through your inbox, responding to basic queries while leaving the more complex ones for your personal touch. It's like having an assistant who works tirelessly, 24/7, ensuring nothing slips through the cracks.

Expanding your service offerings with AI capabilities opens new avenues for income. Why stick to just writing or design when you can offer AI-driven content strategy consultations? Picture yourself as a consultant, advising businesses on how to leverage AI to enhance their digital presence. You bring insights into how AI can optimize their content strategies, boost engagement, and ultimately drive sales. Suddenly, you're not just a freelancer; you're a strategist, helping clients navigate the digital landscape with confidence.

As you explore these opportunities, you might wonder how others have successfully integrated AI into their freelancing careers. Here's a case study that might inspire you: Jane, a freelance writer who expanded her offerings by incorporating AI into her workflow. Initially skeptical about AI's capabilities, Jane soon discovered that by using ChatGPT she could meet tight deadlines without compromising quality. As her confidence grew, so did her client base. She began offering personalized content strategies using AI insights, helping her clients achieve better engagement rates and ROI on their digital campaigns.

Interactive Element: Crafting Your Niche

Take a moment to reflect on how you can integrate AI into your freelancing business. What services could you offer that are enhanced by AI? Jot down three ideas and think about how ChatGPT could assist you in delivering these services efficiently and creatively.

In this ever-evolving digital age, incorporating AI into your freelancing toolkit is not just an advantage; it's becoming essential. You have the chance to elevate your work beyond traditional boundaries, tapping into new markets and delivering services that set you apart from the competition. With tools like ChatGPT at your disposal, the possibilities are endless. As you sip on that latte and listen to the gentle hum of café chatter, remember that in the world of freelancing with AI, you're not just keeping up with the Jones' you're leading the charge in innovation and creativity.

CONSULTING AND COACHING: USING AI TO ENHANCE YOUR SERVICES

Imagine you're a consultant, sipping your morning coffee as you prepare for a client meeting. You've got a mountain of data to analyze, and the clock's ticking. Enter AI analytics tools—your secret weapon in the consulting world. These tools can sift through data faster than you can say "spreadsheet," providing insights that would take days to uncover manually. They help you identify market trends, consumer behavior, and potential opportunities. It's like having a personal analyst whispering the juiciest data points in your ear, making you look like a genius in front of your clients.

Now, let's switch gears to coaching. Personalizing coaching sessions can feel like trying to nail Jell-O to a wall, each client has unique needs that shift over time. AI assessments come to the rescue here, offering personalized coaching plans by analyzing individual preferences, strengths, and areas for improvement. Imagine having a tool that evaluates your client's progress and recommends tailored action steps, ensuring they stay on track and motivated. It's like having a coach for the coach, helping you offer a service that's both effective and deeply personal.

Keeping clients engaged is often easier said than done. We've all had those moments when motivation dips, and progress stalls. AI-driven methods can keep the momentum going. ChatGPT can generate motivational content tailored to your client's needs, offering words of encouragement or new perspectives when they hit a plateau. Think of it as a digital cheerleader, always ready with a pep talk to reignite the spark and keep them moving toward their goals.

On the administrative side of things, AI shines in taking over the mundane tasks that eat up your time. Scheduling meetings can be as tedious as watching paint dry, especially when juggling multiple clients with different time zones. AI-powered scheduling tools optimize meeting times based on availability and preferences, making sure no one gets left hanging. This efficiency frees you up to focus on what truly matters, building relationships and delivering value to your clients.

Textual Element: Case Study

Consider Sarah, a business consultant who was drowning in data and struggling to keep up with client demands. By integrating AI analytics tools into her workflow, she not only streamlined her data analysis process but also discovered new insights that helped her clients achieve their business objectives faster than before. Her client satisfaction skyrocketed, and Sarah found herself with more time to focus on strategic planning rather than number crunching.

Incorporating AI into consulting and coaching services isn't about replacing the human touch; it's about enhancing it. With AI handling the heavy lifting of data analysis and routine tasks, you have more space to connect with clients on a deeper level. You become a guide who navigates complexities with ease, empowering them to reach their full potential while you deliver insights with precision and confidence.

Incorporating AI into your coaching practice isn't about losing the human connection; it's about strengthening it. With AI handling the logistics, you're free to focus on what you do best—connecting with your clients and guiding them toward their goals. You become more than just a coach; you become a partner in their success, armed with tools that enhance your natural abilities.

As you enjoy your morning coffee and dive into the day's work, remember that AI is there to make your life easier. It's like having an extra set of hands, and another brain in your toolkit. Whether you're crunching data or motivating clients, AI helps you deliver top-notch services that keep clients returning for more. Embrace these tools and watch as they transform the way you work, helping you achieve greater heights in your consulting or coaching endeavors.

So there you have it—AI isn't just about robots taking over the world; it's about enhancing how we connect, analyze, and succeed in our professional lives. Whether you're a consultant looking for data-driven insights or a coach personalizing sessions for each client, AI offers solutions that amplify your skills and streamline your processes.

E-COMMERCE AND AI: BOOSTING ONLINE SALES WITH SMART TOOLS

In the bustling world of online shopping, the integration of artificial intelligence is swiftly becoming a game-changer, fundamentally altering and enhancing the e-commerce landscape with its smart capabilities. Imagine leisurely exploring an online store, where a virtual assistant is not merely a tool, but a companion that intuitively understands your needs, often before you even become aware of them. This enchantment is the wizardry of AI, which serves to elevate the customer experience from mundane to extraordinary. These digital assistants, known as chatbots, provide unwavering support around the clock, transforming what might be a bewildering shopping journey into a seamless and enjoyable adventure. Operating without the constraints of time or fatigue, these bots cheerfully handle customer inquiries, ensuring that no shopper feels stranded or ignored. It's kind of like having an endlessly patient shopkeeper whose sole purpose is to enhance your shopping escapade—sans the necessity of coffee breaks.

Moreover, the realm of product recommendations, powered by cutting-edge AI technology, borders on the magical. These systems resemble cunning mind-readers, predicting and suggesting items you might discover you desire, although they hadn't crossed your mind. Through a meticulous analysis of previous purchases and browsing patterns, these recommendation engines tailor the shopping experience to fit individual preferences, greatly boosting customer satisfaction. The outcome is those priceless "aha" instances where a shopper serendipitously stumbles upon exactly what they've been seeking—often when they aren't actively looking for it.

Diving deeper into the logistics of e-commerce, AI emerges as the uncelebrated hero orchestrating the symphony of inventory management. Consider a vast warehouse that appears to possess foresight, timely replenishing its stock just as supplies dwindle. Behind this sorcery lies predictive analytics, the true magician in this performance. By scrutinizing sales trends and historical data, AI can predict future demands with remarkable precision. This strategic foresight eradicates the issue of overburdened shelves or the dreaded "out of stock" notices, allowing retailers to sustain an ideal inventory balance. This balance not only minimizes waste but guarantees that popular items remain perpetually available for immediate dispatch.

When it comes to marketing strategies, AI injects a powerful boost, transforming them into a potent force. Envision email marketing campaigns that feel as personal as a letter from an old friend, yet require minimal human intervention. These digital correspondences are exquisitely timed reminders, arriving in the nick of time to tempt customers with forgotten cart items or bespoke discounts on cherished products. On the dynamic stage of social media, AI tools diligently monitor and analyze engagement, unearthing valuable insights about the advertisements that truly resonate with their audience. It's also like having a marketing savant whispering priceless advice, fine-tuning campaigns to achieve unparalleled influence and reach.

The technological evolution extends to the checkout stage, where AI reimagines the entire process. Picture a buyer reaching the virtual counter with a sense of complete assurance that their transaction will proceed without a hitch. Under the vigilant eyes of AI-driven fraud detection systems, every action is thoroughly scrutinized for signs of suspicious behavior, much like a seasoned detective deducing truths from scant clues. This vigilance ensures transactions are conducted securely and trustworthily, significantly diminishing fraud risks while amplifying consumer trust. Without any procedural glitches, customers glide through the checkout process effortlessly, leaving them with a positive impression and eager to return for future purchases.

Ultimately, the impact of AI on e-commerce is nothing short of revolutionary. It's as if a legion of experts is perpetually laboring in the shadows, fine-tuning every facet of the shopping experience for optimal performance. From elevating customer interactions with tailored personal experiences to perfecting inventory management, from devising intelligent marketing strategies to simplifying the payment processes—AI manages all these intricacies with remarkable finesse. By adopting and integrating these intelligent tools into your e-commerce framework, you find yourself not just treading the path of modern trends, but blazing a trail. This integration places you at the cutting edge, setting new standards for efficiency, customer satisfaction, and business success in the vibrant realm of online commerce.

AI-DRIVEN MARKET RESEARCH: IDENTIFYING TRENDS AND OPPORTUNITIES

What if you had a crystal ball that lets you peek into the future of your industry? That's how AI feels when it comes to market research. AI's ability to process massive datasets is like unleashing a team of supercharged detectives on a mystery, only this time they're uncovering market trends and consumer behaviors. It's like having a backstage pass to the concert of consumer minds, where you get to understand what makes them tick. Through sentiment analysis on social media platforms, AI sifts through the chatter to find out what people are really saying about products, brands, or even the latest viral dance craze. Suddenly, you're not just listening in on conversations; you're decoding them for insights that can shape strategies and guide business decisions.

Competitive analysis takes on a whole new dimension with AI. Imagine having a spyglass that lets you peek into your competitors' playbooks without having to sneak around in the shadows. AI tools provide insights into competitors' strategies and market positioning, generating detailed reports that reveal their activities and how they stack up in the game. It's like having your very own board of advisors whispering industry secrets and helping you stay two steps ahead. These AI-generated reports help you understand not just where the competition stands but also how you can carve out your niche in the market. You're not just playing catch-up; you're setting the pace.

Consumer insight generation becomes an art form with AI at your fingertips. Picture this: you're a detective piecing together clues from customer feedback to create products that truly resonate. With AI's ability to gather and analyze consumer feedback, you can dive deep into the minds of your audience, understanding their needs and desires better than ever before. AI surveys become your magnifying glass, highlighting customer satisfaction insights and areas ripe for improvement. This isn't just about meeting expectations; it's about surpassing them, creating products that make consumers wonder how they ever lived without them.

Predictive market forecasting with AI is like having a weather forecast for your business, only way more accurate. These forecasting tools analyze data to predict future market developments and potential opportunities, giving you a roadmap to navigate the ever-changing landscape. They're like seasoned guides leading you through the wilderness of industry trends, pointing out paths that others might overlook. With AI's help, you're not just reacting to changes; you're anticipating them, ready to seize opportunities before they become mainstream knowledge.

Visual Element: Market Trend Infographic

Consider creating an infographic that visually represents current market trends identified through AI analysis. This could include graphs showcasing consumer sentiment shifts, competitor positioning, and predicted future trends. Such visual aids can help solidify understanding and provide a quick reference guide for strategic planning. 💰

As we gallop further into the world of AI-driven market research, it's clear that these tools don't just provide data—they offer a competitive edge. Whether you're a small business owner looking to carve out your space or a large corporation aiming to maintain dominance, AI empowers you with insights that are actionable and precise. It's like having a Swiss Army knife for market research, ready to adapt and deliver solutions tailored specifically to your needs.

Harnessing these capabilities allows businesses to move from reactive decision-making to proactive strategy development, where informed choices shape the future landscape of industries across the globe. With AI as an ally in market research endeavors, you're not merely participating in the market; you're pioneering new avenues of innovation and growth. As businesses continue integrating these advanced technologies into their operations, the potential for transformative impact becomes increasingly apparent—ushering in an era where informed insights drive success stories yet to be written.

This landscape bristles with opportunities waiting to be explored by those willing to embrace AI's potential fully. As we navigate this brave new world of market research powered by artificial intelligence, remember that understanding consumer behavior is only part of the equation—anticipating trends before they emerge positions businesses at the forefront of innovation.

DEVELOPING DIGITAL PRODUCTS: HOW AI CAN ACCELERATE CREATION

Imagine sitting at your desk, staring at a blank screen, the cursor blinking like it's mocking you. You're about to kick off a new digital product, an app or maybe a nifty piece of software. Here's where AI swoops in like a superhero in a cape. AI doesn't just help you write code; it becomes your coding sidekick. With automated coding suggestions, it's like having a seasoned developer whispering in your ear, suggesting snippets that streamline your work. When bugs creep in, AI debugging tools jump into action, squashing them with precision. It's like having a digital exterminator for your lines of code, ensuring everything runs smoothly.

But what about content? Let's say you're crafting an e-book or developing a course. AI is your creative partner here too. Need a course outline? AI can whip one up faster than you can say "syllabus." It's like having a co-author who never tires, always ready to brainstorm new ideas or expand on existing ones. From generating detailed lesson plans to creating engaging quizzes, AI helps turn your educational vision into reality. You dream it, and AI helps draft and refine it, turning raw ideas into polished products that captivate your audience.

Designing the user interface of your app or software can feel like walking through a maze blindfolded. What works for one user might confuse another. Enter AI's role in user experience improvement. It's like having a team of testers running through every nook and cranny of your interface, spotting potential hiccups before real users ever see them. AI testing tools simulate user interactions, identifying where users might get stuck or frustrated. This feedback loop lets you tweak designs, ensuring a seamless user experience that feels intuitive and natural.

Time-to-market can make or break a digital product. In the fast-paced digital world, speed is everything. This is where AI speeds up product launches like it's got a turbo button. Thanks to AI project management tools, every team member knows exactly what they need to do and when. Tasks are organized, deadlines are clear, and workflows run like a well-oiled machine. Imagine an orchestra where each musician knows their part without missing a beat—that's how AI orchestrates your product launch. No more scrambling at the last minute; AI keeps everything on track, ensuring you hit the market at just the right moment.

AI isn't just about automation; it's about enhancement and efficiency. As you sit there, planning the next steps for your digital product, remember that AI is not just a tool but a partner in innovation. It helps streamline processes that once took hours or even days, freeing you to focus on creativity and strategic thinking. With AI by your side, you're not just keeping up with the competition; you're setting the pace.

In this bustling digital age, AI transforms how we approach product development by offering solutions that were once the stuff of dreams. It's like having an extra pair of hands—or a whole team—

working tirelessly behind the scenes, ensuring every aspect of your product is top-notch. Whether you're developing software or crafting digital content, AI accelerates creation by removing roadblocks and enhancing productivity. As you continue to ride this wave of technology, remember that AI isn't just changing the game; it's redefining it.

Starting off on this tech journey might seem daunting at first, but with AI's assistance, those daunting tasks become manageable. It demystifies complex processes and simplifies workflows. So the next time you're brainstorming your next big digital product idea, imagine how AI can transform your process from start to finish. With its assistance in coding and debugging to content creation and user experience optimization, AI empowers you to innovate confidently and efficiently. As you explore these endless possibilities, let AI guide you through the intricacies of development with ease and finesse.

In this ever-evolving landscape of digital innovation, AI doesn't merely keep pace but propels you forward as a trailblazer in product development. With each advancement in technology comes greater opportunities for creativity and success—so embrace the potential that lies ahead with confidence and enthusiasm!

BUILDING A BRAND WITH AI: PERSONAL BRANDING AND ONLINE PRESENCE

Crafting a unique brand identity in the vast digital expanse can be compared to the thoughtful deliberation of selecting an ensemble for a significant first date. You aim for authenticity, striving to project a genuine image without coming across as contrived or over-polished. Imagine AI tools operating as your ever-imaginative fashion consultant, accompanying you in the digital sphere to artfully design logos and brand materials. These tools can present you with a plethora of creative options, much like a painter's palette, where colors and styles are thoughtfully curated to echo your personal vision and values. This is like having a creative partner who is perpetually brimming with innovative ideas, ensuring that your brand emits an unforgettable essence thatstands out distinctly in a marketplace teeming with competitors, like a crisp, fresh signature scent that lingers gracefully.

Once you have meticulously crafted your visual identity, it becomes essential to amplify your visibility across the digital landscape. Enhancing your online visibility is like to energetically announcing from the digital rooftops, "Hey, look at me!" Advanced AI strategies can significantly augment your online presence, empowering you to reach a broad audience without necessitating a loudspeaker. Search Engine Optimization (SEO) tools adeptly optimize your website's content, ensuring that your brand materializes prominently in search results when potential customers explore themes related to your expertise. Think of it as having an invisible guide gently leading inquisitive gazes to your digital doorstep. In the meantime, AI analytics are your unseen allies diligently tracking the ebb and flow of brand engagement, offering insights into what resonates and what falls flat. It's as if you possess an omniscient observer that listens in on the digital whispers and jubilant cheers of your audience, strategically scattered across the expansive online universe.

ENHANCING ENGAGEMENT THROUGH AI

Engagement transcends mere visibility; it embodies the art of fostering meaningful dialogues. Here, AI assumes a crucial role in nurturing and expanding an attentive online community. Imagine AI chatbots as the frontline ambassadors of your brand, interactively engaging with your audience in real-time. These chatbots are a model of efficiency and dedication, offering round-the-clock service to answer queries or provide support without a hint of fatigue. They ensure that your audience feels acknowledged and appreciated, transforming initial curiosity into steadfast loyalty. It is comparable to having an inexhaustible reserve of eloquence and charisma at your beck and call, ensuring that every interaction leaves a positive and lasting impression.

Yet, what is a brand without the cornerstone of consistency? It would resemble a musical composition that disconcertingly alters pace with every measure—resulting in a bewildered and detached audience. AI emerges as the unsung hero, ensuring that your brand communicates both consistently and cohesively, you could compare it to a skilled conductor orchestrating a harmonious symphony. Tools for content scheduling allow for the consistent dissemination of your narrative across all platforms, preserving the distinct voice of your brand with dependability and fortitude. Envision the satisfaction of scheduling posts weeks in advance, confident in the knowledge that they will resonate harmoniously with your audience. This consistency fosters trust, solidifying your brand identity and clearly articulating your message. It resembles an enthralling story, each chapter seamlessly woven into the next, captivating the hearts and minds of readers from beginning to end.

In concluding this chapter, reflect on the idea that building a brand with AI extends beyond the mere deployment of technology; it encapsulates the endeavor to authentically translate the essence of your individuality into the expansive digital domain. With AI as your trusted ally, you sculpt an identity that not only resonates and engages but also endures with enduring impact. As you venture forward in this book, imagine how these AI-driven branding strategies can be transformative—not merely for your business but also in how you engage and interact with the world at large. Keep these insights close at heart as we transition into the subsequent chapter, where we will delve into leveraging AI for even more dynamic opportunities within your professional landscape that await you with open arms.

6
ADDRESSING ETHICAL CONSIDERATIONS AND AI RESPONSIBILITIES

UNDERSTANDING AI ETHICS: PRIVACY, SECURITY, AND BEYOND

Maybe you are going to a neighborhood block party, you might imagine being surrounded by friends and family, then someone raises the topic of AI ethics. Suddenly, everyone perks up, intrigued yet slightly wary. It's like talking about ghosts—fascinating but a little spooky. So, what exactly is AI ethics all about? Picture it like the moral compass guiding our interactions with artificial intelligence. It ensures we're making fair, transparent, and accountable decisions in this digital age, much like how we try to be decent humans every day.

Defining ethical AI is similar to setting the house rules for a board game—everyone needs to know what's acceptable and what's not. At its core, ethical AI focuses on principles like transparency, accountability, and fairness. Transparency means being clear about how AI systems make their decisions, so no one feels like they're dealing with a mysterious black box. Accountability involves taking responsibility for the technology we create and deploy. It's about owning up when things go wrong and fixing them. Fairness ensures that AI treats everyone equally and without bias, regardless of race, gender, or any other characteristics.

Now, let's chat about privacy—a hot topic in our increasingly connected world. As AI systems become more integrated into our lives, they collect mountains of data about us. Imagine these systems as digital detectives, piecing together clues about our preferences and habits. While this can lead to personalized experiences, it also raises concerns about how our personal information is handled. We've all heard stories of data breaches where sensitive information gets exposed. It's like accidentally leaving your diary open at a party—suddenly, everyone knows your secrets.

Case studies reveal just how serious data breaches can be. For instance, an AI system used in healthcare might inadvertently expose patient records due to a security flaw. Such incidents highlight the importance of robust data protection measures to safeguard privacy. The goal is to ensure that personal information remains confidential and secure, much like locking up valuables in a safe.

Security implications go hand in hand with privacy concerns. Picture AI systems as high-tech vaults that need solid defenses to protect against cybercriminals. These digital bandits constantly seek vulnerabilities to exploit, whether through data theft or unauthorized access. Examples abound of cyberattacks where hackers manipulate AI systems for nefarious purposes. It's sort of like finding a secret passage into a treasure trove—cybercriminals are always on the lookout for weak spots to exploit.

Beyond privacy and security, we must consider broader ethical issues such as the societal impact of AI. Take digital surveillance, for instance. AI-powered cameras can monitor public spaces, raising questions about civil liberties and the balance between security and privacy. It's like having a vigilant but invisible observer watching your every move it may seem comforting for safety but unsettling for personal freedom.

Case Study: The Surveillance Society

Consider a city that deploys AI for extensive surveillance to enhance public safety. While crime rates may drop, citizens express unease over constant monitoring. This case illustrates the ethical dilemma of prioritizing security over privacy and the need for transparent policies that respect individual rights.

With these ethical considerations in mind, it becomes clear that harnessing AI responsibly requires a delicate balance between innovation and moral responsibility. As technology evolves, we must remain vigilant and proactive in addressing these challenges. By doing so, we ensure that AI serves humanity positively and ethically rather than becoming an unchecked force reshaping society without accountability.

Addressing these ethical considerations isn't just about following rules; it's about fostering trust in technology's role in our lives. As we navigate this ever-changing landscape, let's remember that ethical AI is not merely a checkbox but a commitment to doing right by people and society.

DATA SECURITY: PROTECTING YOUR INFORMATION IN AN AI WORLD

There could be a scenario of you sitting comfortably in a bustling café, where the aromatic allure of freshly brewed coffee fills the air, your laptop open in front of you, providing a gateway to the expansive digital universe. As you leisurely sip on your favorite latte, you seamlessly navigate your online experiences: checking emails, engaging in online shopping sprees, and updating your social media status—all effortlessly within arm's reach. However, beneath this surface of convenience lies a pressing concern that demands significant attention: data security. In our rapidly evolving AI-driven era, ensuring the protection of personal and sensitive information has escalated to a level of critical importance, like securing the locks on your home. The situation is starkly alarming: data breaches within AI applications are surging at a rate faster than the frothy foam on your cappuccino. Recent statistics project a grim reality, where breaches have affected millions on an annual basis. It's much like a digital burglary where your cherished personal details are the precious jewels at risk. This elevated risk underscores the necessity of keeping the vault, your data, secured and impregnable from potential threats.

While the notion of safeguarding your information may initially sound daunting, fear not! There exist practical steps that you can take to fortify your data defenses with ease. We begin with the concept of encryption—a sophisticated term describing the art of transforming your data into a concealed, indecipherable code that only the designated, authorized parties can interpret and unlock. Envision it as communicating in an exclusive, secret dialect, decipherable only by your trusted inner circle. By implementing strong, robust encryption techniques, you ensure that even if cyber intruders manage to intercept your data, they would be left scratching their heads, unable to decipher its contents. Imagine a burglar stumbling upon a well-secured safe stacked with confidential documents; without the correct combination, the burglar stands powerless. Regular audits are equally vital within the data security realm, functioning as routine wellness check-ups for your digital assets. These audits ensure compliance with evolving data protection regulations and help in proactively identifying vulnerabilities before they spiral into full-blown crises.

Managing the balance between data access and privacy intricately resembles a tightrope walk; you must provide AI systems with sufficient information to perform optimally while safeguarding personal data's privacy. It's a delicate danc or an intricate tango that encompasses managing user consent and establishing crystal-clear data policies. Picture yourself hosting a vibrant gathering where your guests (AI systems) need just enough information to interact meaningfully without overstepping boundaries into your private domain. User consent management guarantees individuals have ultimate control over their information, affording them the power to determine who can access what data and when. Meanwhile, transparent data policies serve as definitive house rules, outlining the boundaries and expectations for all parties involved, thereby ensuring harmony and mutual respect.

Enter the realm of AI tools specifically designed to amplify and enhance data security measures—your ever-vigilant digital watchdogs standing guard. These tools, empowered by sophisticated algorithms, diligently detect anomalies in data access patterns, akin to how a seasoned detective meticulously deciphers inconsistencies in a suspect's alibi. These AI-driven solutions maintain an unwavering watch over all activities, flagging suspicious behavior and providing alerts long before a security breach can materialize. It's as if you have an indefatigable security guard, who never slumbers, keeping a continuous and vigilant eye over your impregnable data fortress.

Interactive Element: Data Security Checklist

Creating your personalized data security checklist can serve as a proactive stride toward defending your digital life with precision and effectiveness. Start by listing and detailing the encryption techniques currently in use alongside a schedule for regular audits that ensure ongoing compliance with vital data protection regulations. Include a segment detailing the methodologies for managing user consent and establish clear, transparent data policies. This checklist transcends the role of mere task enumeration; it embodies your personal, action-oriented strategy for reinforcing your digital information fortress and enhancing its resilience.

In the contemporary, AI-centric landscape, adopting a proactive stance on data security is far from merely prudent, it's absolutely essential. With the deployment of the right strategies and tools, you can confidently traverse the digital frontier, assured in the knowledge that your information remains fortified and implicitly secure. You could even compare it to the esteemed Fort Knox. As you leisurely sip your next invigorating latte and delve into the digital realm, you can rest at ease knowing that you've established robust, unyielding defenses that vigilantly guard your valuable data.

THE HUMAN ELEMENT: MAINTAINING EMPATHY IN AI INTERACTIONS

Think of AI as an eager but sometimes clueless friend who just doesn't get the hint when you're feeling down. You know, that buddy who keeps talking about the weather while you're having a minor existential crisis? That's where empathy comes in, the secret sauce that makes AI feel a touch more human, a virtual ingredient that adds warmth to the otherwise sterile realm of machine interactions. In this digital age, maintaining empathy in AI interactions is crucial. It ensures that when you talk to your virtual assistant about your cat's latest escapade, it responds appropriately, perhaps even with a dash of humor or a sprinkle of understanding. Empathy in AI isn't just about making machines more relatable; it's about crafting meaningful and supportive engagements that prevent interactions from feeling as though you've just spoken to a well-dressed butler devoid of emotional range, one who politely holds the door open but lacks the warmth to ask how your day went.

Yet, let's not kid ourselves, AI still faces significant challenges in interpreting emotional cues accurately. Imagine telling your digital assistant, "I'm so over today," a phrase loaded with weary connotation, and instead of offering comforting words or an encouraging nudge, it nonchalantly suggests buying a new calendar, missing the weight of your lamentation entirely. AI's potential to misinterpret emotional nuances is a notable hurdle, difficult indeed to explain sarcasm to a robot with a literal comprehension; it just doesn't compute. This misinterpretation can lead to frustrating interactions, where the AI response feels mechanical rather than genuinely understanding, evoking an exasperated sigh from the user. When it comes to designing AI systems, developers need to intently focus on embedding empathy into the algorithms, a process that involves training AI models on vast and diverse datasets which can effectively recognize varied emotional expressions and subtleties. Just like how you gradually learn to read a friend's mood through years of friendship and shared experiences, AI needs considerable exposure to a wide spectrum of emotions to genuinely understand human feelings and adequately respond.

To strike a harmonious balance between automation and empathy, we must explore and implement ways to retain the human touch even within automated systems. Consider hybrid models that skillfully combine AI with human customer service, merging efficiency with empathy. Picture this: you're calling customer support, greeted first by an AI assistant that adeptly handles routine queries with precision and speed, seamlessly transitioning you to a human agent when your issue requires the nuanced understanding that only a human can provide. These hybrid systems ensure operational efficiency without sacrificing the warmth and understanding that only human interaction can provide. It would be like being served by an automated teller at your favorite local café who always gets your order right yet still engages you with a reassuring, friendly smile Part of the experience of the cafe is the relational connection and memory.

There are already some impressive examples of empathetic AI applications currently in use. Take mental health support systems, for instance. These AI-powered platforms offer compassionate responses to individuals seeking help, thoughts filled with caring nuances. Imagine reaching out to a virtual counselor during a difficult time, only to receive thoughtful and comforting messages that genuinely make you feel heard, understood, and supported at a level that technology often struggles to achieve. These systems are meticulously designed with empathy as their foundation, offering support devoid of judgment and creating a safe, inclusive space for users to transparently express themselves.

Incorporating empathy into AI interactions isn't only about rendering conversations more pleasant; it's fundamentally about fostering genuine connections between technology and humans. When we prioritize empathy in AI design, we unleash the potential to create systems that not only accomplish tasks efficiently but also profoundly resonate with users on an emotional level. Think of ChatGPT as having a digital friend who's always present to lend an ear or offer encouraging words no matter the circumstance, a presence that doesn't merely exist to serve, but one that listens and empathizes.

As we continue to explore and expand the potential of AI, it's vital to keep in mind the significance of empathy in shaping these interactions. It's about transcending algorithms and data; it's about grasping the human experience in its entirety and creating technology that not only complements it but enhances it. By wholeheartedly embracing empathy, we can build AI systems that offer support in genuinely meaningful ways, bridging the chasm between man and machine with heart and profound understanding. This journey towards empathetic AI isn't just about potential technological advancement; it's about crafting companionship across realms, digital and human alike, with empathy as our guide.

AI BIAS AND FAIRNESS: ENSURING EQUITABLE TECHNOLOGY USE

Picture this: you're scrolling through a social media feed, and you notice a post about AI and bias. You might think, "Bias? In my AI?

Surely not!" But let's face it we notice bias creeps up like that one relative who always shows up unannounced at family gatherings. It's not that AI suddenly woke up one day and decided to be biased; rather, it reflects the data and decisions that humans have fed into it. Imagine facial recognition technology, for instance, which, despite its sleek appearance, often stumbles when identifying individuals with darker skin tones. This isn't just a tech hiccup; it's a significant problem with real-world consequences. Misidentification can lead to wrongful arrests or accusations, especially when law enforcement depends on these systems.

So, how do we tackle this sneaky specter of bias lurking in AI systems? A good start is by diversifying the datasets we use to train these models. Think of it like assembling a jigsaw puzzle; if you only have pieces that fit one part of the picture, you'll never see the whole image. By including diverse data that represents various communities and backgrounds, we give AI a fighting chance to understand the world more equitably. It's about teaching AI to recognize all the colors in the crayon box, not just its favorite shade.

Fairness in AI deployment isn't just a nice-to-have; it's crucial across sectors. Imagine applying for a job only to find out an algorithm decided you weren't the right fit based on biased data. It's like being judged by a robot that doesn't speak your language, or worse, speaks it but doesn't understand you. Ensuring fairness in hiring algorithms is vital to prevent discrimination and promote equal opportunities. It's about leveling the playing field so everyone gets a fair shot, regardless of their background. Now the tools are available to anyone, and you too can make money from anywhere.

You might wonder how transparency plays into this. Well, imagine if every decision made by AI came with a little pop-up explaining the "why" behind it. That's what we mean by explainable AI models, it makes sure you can peek behind the curtain to see how decisions are made. This transparency fosters trust and accountability, turning AI from a mysterious black box into something more approachable and understandable. It's like having a GPS that not only tells you where to turn but explains why it's choosing that route.

The discussion around AI bias and fairness isn't just for techies or philosophers; it's for everyone who interacts with technology—which is pretty much all of us. By addressing these issues head-on, we can create systems that reflect our best intentions rather than our subconscious prejudices. It's about making sure technology serves everyone fairly, providing equal opportunities and outcomes. Just think of it as housecleaning for our digital future tidying up biases and ensuring everything's in order.

With these practices in mind, we can strive toward a more equitable technological landscape where AI supports rather than stumbles over diversity. It's about building systems that recognize the full spectrum of human experience, ensuring everyone has a seat at the table—no matter who they are or where they come from. And as we continue to navigate this digital age, let's remember that fairness isn't just a checkbox but a cornerstone for building trust in technology's role in our lives.

So, next time you interact with AI, consider how fairness and bias play into the equation. It's not just about algorithms; it's about people—like you and me—living in a world increasingly shaped by technology. By focusing on equity today, we can help shape a future where everyone benefits from technological progress without leaving anyone behind.

RESPONSIBLE AI USE: GUIDELINES FOR ETHICAL INTERACTION

Pretend you're sitting in a cozy coffee shop, sipping your favorite brew, when the topic of responsible AI use pops up. Suddenly, you're the center of attention, not because of your latte art skills, but because everyone is curious about what responsible AI interaction actually means. It's like explaining the rules of a new board game to your friends—the goal is to ensure everyone understands and plays by the same principles. Establishing ethical guidelines for AI is about creating a framework that ensures technology serves us fairly and transparently. Picture these guidelines as the rulebook for AI development and deployment, focusing on principles like transparency and accountability. It's about ensuring that AI systems are designed with these principles in mind, much like crafting a recipe where each ingredient plays a crucial part in the final dish.

Now, let's talk about user responsibilities in AI interactions. Think of it like being a good neighbor—being mindful and respectful of others' boundaries. When engaging with AI, users have a role to play in ensuring ethical interactions. This includes adhering to consent protocols and respecting privacy settings. It's like knocking before entering someone's room or asking before borrowing their stuff. By following these protocols, users help maintain an environment where AI can function ethically and effectively, ensuring personal boundaries are respected in this digital age.

On the corporate side of things, companies have a massive role in promoting ethical AI use. Imagine a company as a big family where everyone needs to pitch in to keep things running smoothly. Corporations need to establish policies that advocate for ethical practices and compliance. It's about setting standards that ensure AI systems are developed responsibly. These policies act like the family rules everyone agrees on, aimed at maintaining harmony and integrity within the AI landscape.

Ethical dilemmas in AI are inevitable, much like those tricky situations in life where you're caught between a rock and a hard place. How do we navigate these dilemmas? Consider exploring decision-making processes as akin to mapping out a route on a road trip—sometimes, you'll hit detours or unexpected roadblocks. Case studies provide valuable insights into these challenges. Imagine an AI developer facing an ethical conundrum: should they prioritize speed or fairness? These real-world scenarios offer lessons on how to approach complex decisions, balancing ethical considerations with practical outcomes.

Interactive Element: Ethical Decision-Making Exercise

Anything could happen, garbage in, garbage out as they say. What if you're the architect of an AI system tasked with automating hiring processes for a company. You've just discovered that the system may be biased against certain groups of applicants based on incomplete data. What steps would you take to address this? Would you halt deployment until biases are fixed? Consider documenting your thought process and proposed solutions.

Providing a framework for responsible AI use isn't just about setting rules; it's about fostering an environment where technology enhances rather than hinders our lives. It's about making sure everyone involved in the creation and use of AI—developers, companies, users—plays their part in maintaining ethical standards. By doing so, we ensure that AI not only adheres to best practices but also contributes positively to society.

As we continue to integrate AI into our lives, these guidelines act as our compass, guiding us toward ethical interactions that respect individual rights and promote fairness. They remind us that technology serves us best when developed and used with integrity and mindfulness. Through conscious engagement with these principles, we can create an AI ecosystem that benefits all stakeholders involved.

Each interaction with AI is an opportunity to reinforce these values, ensuring that as technology evolves, it does so with respect for humanity at its core. By embracing responsible AI use, we pave the way for a future where technology seamlessly supports our aspirations while upholding the ethical principles that define our shared human experience.

In this ever-evolving digital landscape, let's strive to use AI responsibly—like a good friend who knows when to listen and when to speak up—ensuring our technological companions enhance rather than detract from our lives.

THE FUTURE OF AI: NAVIGATING ETHICAL CHALLENGES AHEAD

Picture this: in the quiet solitude of your morning routine, you're casually sipping your morning coffee. As you read through the latest news updates, an article catches your eye, causing you to pause for thought. It's centered around AI's increasingly significant role within autonomous weapon systems. In an instant, your imagination is flooded with vivid images of robotic figures straight out of dystopian sci-fi films, but these aren't just figments of fiction. They are tangible possibilities that warrant serious consideration. These futuristic scenarios underscore a crucial point—while AI technology propels us toward unprecedented advancements, it simultaneously presents us with a labyrinth of ethical challenges that we cannot afford to overlook. The implications aren't just plotlines for a blockbuster film or novel; they represent real-world quandaries demanding our urgent attention. As AI increasingly permeates military applications, the questions of accountability, responsibility, and control come sharply into focus. We are left to ponder critically: Who holds the authority to make decisions on the usage of such sophisticated systems, and under what circumstances? This is a pressing topic that necessitates profound thought and rigorous debate.

As we witness AI technology advancing at an extraordinary pace, our ethical frameworks must evolve accordingly to keep pace with these developments. In many ways, it's analogous to attempting to retrofit a jet engine into the confines of a bicycle; adhering to outdated guidelines will no longer suffice. Just as our gadgets require constant updates to function effectively, our ethical standards need regular revisitation and revision to maintain their relevance. We cannot perceive this endeavor as a singular task; instead, it demands ongoing attention and continuous effort. Imagine approaching our ethical frameworks in much the same way as we handle updates on our smartphones—constantly upgrading to fix glitches and enhance overall functionality. Remaining stagnant isn't an option when we stand at the threshold of such high stakes. Our ethical compass mandates regular calibration, enabling us to navigate this constantly shifting technological landscape with precision and confidence.

Here's the critical insight: addressing these ethical dilemmas isn't a solitary endeavor—it's one that requires unyielding teamwork on a global scale. No single nation or entity can bear the responsibility of tackling these multifaceted challenges alone. It's akin to attempting to construct a bridge with only half the required components; advancement is impossible without unified effort. Therefore, fostering international cooperation is imperative to establish universal standards for ethical AI utilization. Picture a conceptualized 'United Nations for AI ethics'—a global platform where nations convene to negotiate and agree on foundational principles that guide technology to serve humanity's collective interests. Initiatives committed to nurturing international agreements and standards are paramount in this mission, offering a common lexicon for safeguarding ethical AI implementation across geopolitical borders.

So, how do we systematically prepare for the ethical future of AI? Embracing proactivity is the linchpin. We cannot afford to adopt a passive stance, hoping for favorable outcomes. Urgent action is required. Spearheading interdisciplinary research in the domain of AI ethics marks a commendable starting point. By amalgamating the expertise of professionals from diverse realms—technologists, ethicists, and policymakers alike—a holistic approach to solving these issues is forged. Think of it as assembling an all-encompassing superhero team, where each member contributes their distinctive skills and insights, poised to overcome any forthcoming challenges with finesse and determination.

As we draw this chapter to a close, it's essential to remember that the future of AI transcends mere fascination with shiny new gadgets or the allure of groundbreaking innovations. Instead, it's about aligning these advancements with our foundational values and principles. As we continue traversing the expansive landscape of AI's potential, we must steadfastly maintain our focus on sculpting a future where technology acts to enhance human existence, firmly upholding our ethical standards. This isn't simply about equipping ourselves for what's ahead; it's about actively shaping and steering it. By prioritizing responsibility and unyielding collaboration, we can deftly navigate the ethical challenges that lie ahead, all the while safeguarding humanity's paramount interests.

As we now turn the page to delve into how AI can revolutionize industries, let's carry forward the invaluable lessons acquired here—embracing technology with both eager anticipation and prudent caution, thereby ensuring it serves as a catalyst for good in our rapidly evolving world.

7
CONTINUING YOUR AI EDUCATION AND STAYING UPDATED

THE LIFELONG LEARNER: CULTIVATING AN AI LEARNING MINDSET

Picture this scenario: you're attending a lively potluck dinner, surrounded by a diverse group of fascinating individuals, and the conversation turns to the captivating world of AI innovations. You find yourself nodding politely, smiling along with the discussion, yet somewhere in the recesses of your mind, a small voice wonders if you should have brought an engaging book on artificial intelligence rather than your delectable, well-known spaghetti dish. If this situation resonates with you, rest assured—you are not alone. Embracing a lifelong learning mindset is the key to transforming those uneasy moments from anxious struggles to opportunities for empowerment. Let's be candid with ourselves: AI knowledge resembles the universe in its complexity and propensity for expansion—it is continuously growing and changing. The information you grasp today might evolve drastically by tomorrow, making it imperative that you maintain an insatiably curious and adaptable approach as your most powerful resource.

Rather than perceiving this ceaseless transformation as a source of intimidation, reframe each new challenge as a chance to develop further. Think of it as an endless scavenger hunt, where each intriguing clue you uncover brings you one step closer to an intricate understanding of this phenomenon.

Now, let us turn to the concept of goal setting, an essential aspect akin to mapping out your route while preparing for a road trip—you need a clear direction to guide your path. Begin with modest, short-term objectives. Perhaps you aim to gain insights into basic AI principles, or you're curious about understanding how innovations like ChatGPT interpret and process language. These short-term goals act as your pit stops along the journey, providing gratifying successes that boost your confidence. Following this, extend your aspirations to more long-term ambitions. Envision building an expert-level proficiency in AI applications or maybe even spearheading a groundbreaking project at work. These long-term goals are like captivating destination points that keep your spirit motivated through prolonged periods of learning.

Consistency emerges as the cornerstone when mastering new skills. It's not about the frantic last-minute cram session before an important presentation—it's about weaving learning seamlessly into the fabric of your daily routine. Carve out specific time slots for AI education, whether it's during your quiet morning ritual with coffee or as part of your wind-down regimen at night. The use of habit-tracking apps can be incredibly beneficial as they function like personal cheerleaders, gently urging you onward, even when motivation wanes. As incorporating learning into your daily routine becomes second nature, absorbing information becomes smoother, facilitating the creation of meaningful connections.

Curiosity serves as your steadfast compass throughout this journey. As you navigate the boundless world of AI, let your interests guide you. Perhaps you find yourself captivated by AI's potential to craft poetical works or its newfound ability to predict market fluctuations with surprising accuracy. Engage in projects closely aligned with these passions. Experiment with AI tools or undertake a small project that resonates with your interests, whether it centers around photography, finance, or another field entirely. Such proactive pursuits may unveil unexpected insights and ignite innovation in surprising ways, possibly leading you down paths previously unexplored.

Reflection Exercise: Your AI Curiosity Map

Take a deliberate moment to jot down the aspects of AI that spark your interest. Are you drawn to natural language processing, or are autonomous vehicles where your curiosity lies? Use this list as a developing map, guiding where you aim to delve deeper. As your exploration continues, actively note each new concept mastered and any emerging questions needing answers. This exercise serves the dual purpose of keeping your curiosity thriving while also providing a tangible representation of your intellectual expansion.

In summary, adopting a growth mindset, setting realistic yet motivating goals, and maintaining steady habits are key to transforming learning from a daunting endeavor into an exciting adventure. Remember, an expert was once an enthusiastic beginner who persevered through challenges. You are not alone on this discovery path—an abundance of resources and supportive communities await to aid you in your knowledge-seeking journey.

As your journey in the incredible realm of AI progresses, keep your sense of wonder, freely ask questions, and never hesitate to seek assistance when necessary. The technological landscape is vast and formidable, yet with an open mind and boundless willingness to learn, you'll traverse it with the finesse of an experienced explorer, unearthing hidden treasures at every twist and turn.

TOP RESOURCES FOR AI ENTHUSIASTS: BOOKS, COURSES, AND MORE

Imagine being in a library, surrounded by the soothing scent of old pages. Books are key to understanding AI, with "Artificial Intelligence: A Guide to Intelligent Systems" by Michael Negnevitsky providing an approachable introduction to concepts, like having a friendly professor. "Life 3.0" by Max Tegmark explores AI's societal impact, encouraging contemplation about our future with AI. These are not just for tech enthusiasts but also for anyone curious about AI's role in life.

Switch to online courses for an interactive learning experience. Imagine enjoying coffee while attending Andrew Ng's "AI for Everyone" on Coursera. It's like having a guide simplifying AI concepts, making them digestible for everyone. Udacity's AI Programming with Python Nanodegree is a brain boot camp, equipping you with essential AI skills. These courses deliver practical, applicable skills. It also helps you feel the community support of new challenges.

For auditory learners, podcasts like "The AI Alignment Podcast" provide expert insights during activities such as jogging. Visually inclined learners will find channels like "3Blue1Brown" on YouTube creatively present AI concepts through inviting animations.

Delving deeper, academic papers offer a treasure of cutting-edge research, available on platforms like arXiv. Though dense initially, they reveal insights into advancements that shape AI’s future.

The Role of AI Conferences and Workshops in Your Journey

Some of the events where innovation fuels the atmosphere are crazy to attend.. AI conferences provide opportunities to learn from industry leaders. Networking naturally occurs as you engage with peers sharing your AI enthusiasm.

Conferences like NeurIPS offer insights into cutting-edge research, while The AI Summit addresses practical applications transforming industries. Both academic and commercial interests find representation at such events.

Virtual conferences allow global participation, while in-person workshops offer hands-on learning. Maximize conference benefits by preparing—research speakers and relevant session content. Active participation through inquiries and discussions enhances learning and cultivates valuable connections in the AI field.

JOINING THE AI COMMUNITY: NETWORKING AND SUPPORT GROUPS

Think about when you might attend a lively gathering, buzzing with excitement, where everyone's as eager to chat about AI as they are about their favorite TV shows. That's the vibe you get when you dive into the world of AI communities. It's like finding your tribe, where you can share your geeky enthusiasm without judgment. Engaging with others in this space brings a treasure trove of benefits. You gain insights from diverse experiences, swap stories about AI successes and challenges, and maybe even stumble upon that elusive solution you've been searching for. Imagine AI forums as cozy campfires where knowledge is shared, questions are welcome, and everyone contributes their unique perspective. The camaraderie is tangible, and the connections you make could lead to collaborations, mentorships, or even friendships.

Online platforms offer the perfect venue to connect with fellow AI enthusiasts without leaving the comfort of your couch. Reddit's r/MachineLearning is a bustling hub where discussions unfold, news is shared, and curious minds converge. It's like a digital café where you can sip your coffee while soaking in the latest AI trends. For those seeking professional connections, LinkedIn hosts AI-specific groups that cater to various interests. These groups are not just about networking; they're about learning from industry experts, staying updated on breakthroughs, and exploring potential career opportunities. Engaging with these online communities is like having a virtual water cooler chat with peers who understand your passion for AI.

But don't stop at your screen—real-world meetups offer a dynamic dimension to your AI journey. Picture attending a local AI meetup through Meetup.com, where you're surrounded by like-minded individuals eager to exchange ideas and insights. These events provide a platform for face-to-face interactions that can lead to meaningful collaborations. Whether you're attending workshops to learn new skills or simply engaging in thought-provoking discussions, these gatherings are fertile ground for expanding your network and broadening your perspective.

Mentorship is the secret sauce that elevates your AI endeavors to new heights. Seeking guidance from experienced professionals can provide invaluable insights and personalized advice tailored to your goals. Platforms like MentorCruise connect you with mentors who understand the nuances of navigating the AI landscape. Imagine having a mentor as your personal guide, helping you navigate challenges, offering feedback on projects, and providing encouragement when the going gets tough. The mentorship journey is like having a wise sage by your side, helping you unlock your potential and charting a course toward success.

Engaging in these communities isn't just about learning—it's about creating a support network that fuels your passion for AI. It's about finding camaraderie with individuals who share your curiosity and drive. The AI community becomes a place where you can exchange ideas, brainstorm solutions, and celebrate achievements together. Whether you're seeking technical advice or simply want to share a funny AI meme, these connections offer a sense of belonging in the ever-evolving world of artificial intelligence.

Networking within the AI community isn't just about professional growth—it's about enriching your understanding of this dynamic field. By immersing yourself in discussions, attending events, and seeking mentorship, you're not just gaining knowledge; you're building relationships that can have a lasting impact on your journey. The connections you make today might lead to collaborative projects tomorrow or even lifelong friendships.

As you navigate this landscape of networking and support groups, keep an open mind and embrace the diverse perspectives you'll encounter. Every conversation is an opportunity to learn something new, challenge assumptions, and broaden your horizons. The community becomes more than just a collection of individuals—it becomes a tapestry woven from shared experiences and collective growth.

So whether you're diving into online forums, attending local meetups, or seeking mentorship guidance, remember that you're not alone on this path. The AI community welcomes you with open arms, ready to explore the endless possibilities that artificial intelligence has to offer.

STAYING INFORMED: FOLLOWING AI TRENDS WITHOUT OVERWHELM

Picture this: you're sitting with a hot cup of coffee, ready to dive into the vast ocean of AI information. But instead of drowning in a sea of endless articles, you can create a personalized information feed that feels more like a gentle stream. Imagine an RSS feed as your personal assistant, gathering all the AI news that matters to you. It's like having a digital librarian who knows exactly what you're interested in. By choosing specific topics and sources, you can tailor your feed to your preferences. This way, you're not bombarded with irrelevant information, and you can focus on what truly piques your curiosity.

When it comes to consuming information, less is often more. Prioritize quality over quantity by choosing reputable sources known for their reliable reporting on AI trends. Think of it like selecting the finest ingredients for a recipe—you want the best to create something truly delightful. By focusing on trusted sources, you avoid misinformation and gain a deeper understanding of the AI landscape. It might be tempting to read everything out there, but being selective ensures you're not overwhelmed by a flood of data. Instead, you're sipping from a curated glass of knowledge.

Let's talk about consistency. Setting aside regular times for catching up on AI developments is like having a standing coffee date with a dear friend. Whether it's once a week or every other week, scheduling these moments ensures you're keeping up without feeling rushed. It gives you the opportunity to dive deep into topics of interest and reflect on what you've learned. Imagine it as a leisurely stroll through a garden of ideas, allowing you to appreciate each bloom without feeling hurried.

Now, let's address the elephant in the room: information overload. It's easy to get overwhelmed when you're constantly bombarded with new articles, updates, and notifications. To manage this, set limits on your daily tech-related reading time. Think of it as setting boundaries with a chatty neighbor who knows all the gossip—you enjoy the conversation but need space to process it all. By allocating specific times for reading and sticking to them, you prevent burnout and ensure you're absorbing information at a comfortable pace.

A strategy that works wonders is creating a dedicated space for your AI updates. Perhaps it's your favorite reading nook or a cozy corner in your home office. This space becomes your sanctuary for learning, free from distractions and interruptions. It's where you can dive into articles, watch informative videos, and even jot down notes or reflections on what you've discovered. Creating this space helps you associate learning with relaxation and enjoyment, making it something you look forward to rather than another task on your to-do list.

Another tip is to balance digital consumption with offline activities. After you've absorbed a wealth of information, step away from the screen and let your mind wander. Go for a walk, engage in a hobby, or simply sit in silence. These moments allow your brain to process what you've learned and make connections you might not have considered before. It's like letting dough rise after kneading—giving it time to expand and develop before baking it into something delicious.

Finally, remember to embrace the joy of discovery. Learning about AI trends doesn't have to be a chore; it can be an adventure filled with "aha" moments and exciting revelations. Approach each piece of information with curiosity, allowing yourself to be surprised by what you uncover. Whether it's a groundbreaking innovation or an insightful analysis, these discoveries enrich your understanding and keep your passion for AI alive.

Staying informed about AI trends doesn't mean drowning in data; it means curating your experience to suit your interests and lifestyle. By crafting a personalized information feed, prioritizing quality sources, setting regular update times, and managing information intake mindfully, you're equipped to navigate the ever-evolving world of AI without feeling overwhelmed.

THE ROLE OF AI CONFERENCES AND WORKSHOPS IN YOUR JOURNEY

Just imagine being at a bustling conference hall, the air buzzing with excitement and the hum of voices discussing the latest in AI. Attending AI conferences is like stepping into a treasure trove of knowledge and ideas, offering a golden opportunity to network with industry experts. Picture this: you're at a coffee stand, latte in hand, and you find yourself chatting with a leading AI researcher who casually drops a nugget of wisdom that sparks a revolutionary idea for your next project. These events are more than just gatherings;

they're melting pots of innovation, where you can rub shoulders with the best minds in the field and glean insights that you won't find in textbooks or online courses.

Let's talk about some top-notch conferences you might consider attending. NeurIPS (Neural Information Processing Systems) is an absolute must for anyone interested in cutting-edge research. It's where the latest breakthroughs are unveiled, from advancements in machine learning to novel computational models. Imagine it as a dazzling expo of ideas, with researchers presenting their findings and sparking discussions that could shape the future of AI. On the other hand, The AI Summit caters to those more inclined toward business applications. Here, you'll encounter how AI is transforming industries, from healthcare to finance, offering a pragmatic view of how AI is applied in real-world scenarios. These conferences are like lighthouses guiding you through the vast sea of AI possibilities, illuminating paths you might not have considered before.

Now, let's weigh the benefits of virtual versus in-person events. Virtual conferences offer flexibility, allowing you to soak in knowledge from the comfort of your home. You can attend sessions from around the globe without worrying about travel expenses or time zones. It's like having a ticket to every corner of the world without leaving your couch. However, there's something irreplaceable about attending in person. The energy in the room, hands-on workshops, and spontaneous interactions create an atmosphere where learning leaps off the screen and into reality. You can't replicate the experience of discussing ideas face-to-face or participating in interactive sessions where you can try out new technologies firsthand.

To make the most of these events, preparation is key. Before attending, delve into the conference agenda and research the speakers and topics that pique your interest. Think of it as planning a road trip—you'll want to map out the must-see stops along your journey. This way, you can prioritize sessions that align with your goals and interests. Consider drafting questions or topics you'd like to explore further; this proactive approach will enable you to engage meaningfully during Q&A sessions or networking breaks. And don't forget to bring plenty of business cards or prepare your LinkedIn profile for new connections—networking is one of the most valuable aspects of conference attendance.

Remember, conferences aren't just about absorbing information—they're about sharing your passion and ideas with others. Don't hesitate to strike up conversations with fellow attendees, whether they're seasoned professionals or fellow enthusiasts just starting their AI journey. These interactions often lead to unexpected collaborations or insights that could prove invaluable down the line. And if you're feeling a bit shy, think of conferences as a safe space where everyone shares a common interest: the fascinating world of artificial intelligence.

So, whether you're attending virtually or physically, be open to new experiences and embrace every opportunity to learn and connect. Conferences and workshops are like masterclasses in AI exploration, offering a wealth of knowledge and networking possibilities that can propel your understanding and career to new heights.

Balancing AI Learning with a Busy Schedule: Tips and Tricks

Let's face it, life can often feel like a juggling act, especially when you're trying to squeeze in some AI learning amidst work meetings, grocery shopping, and the occasional attempt at exercise. But fear not! There are ways to fit learning into even the busiest of schedules. One effective strategy is time-blocking. It's like reserving a VIP section in your calendar just for AI study. You choose a dedicated slot each week where you focus solely on learning, turning off phone notifications and any other distractions. Imagine this time as your personal sanctuary for uninterrupted study, where the only thing on the agenda is diving deeply into AI concepts. Whether it's early mornings with a steaming cup of coffee or late nights when the world quiets down and the stars twinkle outside your window, find a time that suits you best and stick to it. This sacred time becomes a cherished part of your routine, where complex ideas unravel and curiosity takes flight, leaving you energized rather than exhausted.

Embrace the Power of Micro-Learning

Now, let's talk about micro-learning—those little pockets of time you can exploit to absorb knowledge. Picture yourself waiting for your morning latte or sitting in traffic (as a passenger, of course). These moments are perfect for quick yet impactful learning sessions. Plug into an AI podcast during your commute, enveloping yourself in thought-provoking discussions that deepen your understanding. Alternatively, watch short video tutorials while you wait for dinner to cook, turning a routine task into an opportunity for enrichment. It's like snacking on knowledge throughout the day, providing a steady stream of information that incrementally builds and cements your understanding over time. These bite-sized pieces of information gradually build up and enhance your understanding over time, much like a sculptor chiseling away at marble to reveal the form within.

Set Realistic Learning Goals

Setting realistic learning goals is another crucial element in keeping your AI journey manageable and fulfilling. We all love the idea of becoming an overnight AI expert, mastering sophisticated algorithms with ease. However, setting smaller, more achievable objectives can be much more effective and satisfying. Break down larger topics into digestible segments, focusing on one aspect at a time. Maybe this week you delve into the intricacies of machine learning algorithms, exploring their mathematical foundations and practical applications. The following week, you might tackle neural networks, uncovering their layers and learning how they mimic the problem-solving processes of the human brain. This progressive approach keeps you from feeling overwhelmed and allows for steady progress, like piecing together a complex puzzle one small, satisfying piece at a time.

Infuse Learning into Everyday Tasks

Incorporating AI learning into daily life is more about creativity than complexity. Consider using AI-powered language apps to build vocabulary or knowledge while performing mundane household chores or running errands. Imagine practicing your Spanish or French via AI while folding laundry or tidying up the kitchen, transforming these ordinary tasks into interactive learning experiences. This seamless integration makes learning feel less like a chore and more like an enjoyable and enriching part of your routine. Suddenly, you discover that you're not just multitasking; you're wisely enhancing your everyday activities with new knowledge, turning downtime into opportunities for growth.

Achieving Harmony Between Curiosity and Commitments

As we wrap up this chapter, remember that balancing AI learning with a busy schedule doesn't require drastic changes or a complete overhaul of your lifestyle. Instead, it's about finding harmony between your commitments and your natural curiosity for AI. With these tips and tricks in your arsenal, you'll be equipped to weave learning seamlessly into your day-to-day life without feeling like you're sacrificing precious free time. These strategies empower you to embrace lifelong learning as a fulfilling journey, rather than a burdensome task.

In the grand scheme of things, each small step you take brings you closer to a deeper understanding of AI, equipping you with invaluable skills for both personal and professional growth. As we continue to explore this fascinating world of artificial intelligence, keep an eye out for opportunities to apply what you've learned in real-world scenarios. Up next, we'll delve into how AI can be leveraged to create remote income opportunities, providing practical ways to make money from anywhere. Stay curious and open-minded as we journey onward, embracing the endless possibilities that arise from merging advanced technology with human creativity!

8

EMBRACING THE FUTURE: AI TRENDS AND INNOVATIONS

◆BEYOND CHATGPT: THE NEXT GENERATION OF CONVERSATIONAL AI

IMAGINE for a moment that you are sitting at a bustling café, surrounded by the hum of lively conversation. You find yourself captivated, eavesdropping on a conversation so engaging that for a moment, you forget your coffee cooling beside you. Now picture this: the lively exchange isn't between two people, but rather between you and your AI assistant. This scenario isn't just a futuristic reverie; it is swiftly becoming our reality. As artificial intelligence technology continues to advance at a rapid pace, we are progressing beyond the capabilities of ChatGPT and into an era where conversational AI models are not only more sophisticated and nuanced but also finely tuned to recognize and respond to the emotional subtleties and multilingual demands of users like never before. These new-generation AI systems are designed to go beyond simply comprehending the words you utter; they delve deeper into understanding the "how" and "why" that form the complex tapestry of our communication.

Exploring the intricacies of these next-gen conversational models is akin to embarking on a journey into a world where traditional language barriers slowly begin to dissolve. These AI models don't limit themselves to speaking English alone; they switch effortlessly between languages, whether it's parlez-vous Français, hablan Español, or any other tongue. Such multilingual capabilities afford an unparalleled ability to offer real-time translation during conversations, smoothing the path for global communications as they breeze across linguistic divides. Visualize planning an exciting trip to Paris, where your AI companion not only translates dialogues with locals instantaneously but does so with cultural sensitivity. This phenomenon transcends the literal aspects of language—it is about interweaving different cultures into a harmonious tapestry of understanding and connection. Equally revolutionary is the incorporation of emotional intelligence in AI. This transformative capability enables AI tools to discern and respond to emotional cues, evolving ordinary chats into deeply engaging dialogues characterized by empathy and resonance.

Ever changing features in conversational AI continue to reshape and redefine our interactions with technology. Consider, for example, those awkward moments we've all experienced when trying to communicate in a language foreign to us, and then imagine the ease as your AI steps into the role of an amiable sidekick, translating with the finesse of a local guide. It's akin to carrying around a pocket translator infused with all the charm and knowledge a seasoned local might provide. These remarkable advancements represent more than spectacular feats of engineering; they are driving a paradigm shift in how we experience the world, tearing down communication barriers and significantly enriching the quality of cross-cultural interactions.

It's no revelation that the realm of customer experience is being fundamentally transformed thanks to the endless possibilities of conversational AI. Gone are the days dominated by interminable hold times and droning robotic voices. In their place, we find personalized interactions that come across as being both genuine and remarkably human-like. Imagine, if you will, calling a customer service hotline and feeling as though you're conversing with an insightful friend who intuitively understands your unique needs and preferences. The depth of personalization extends beyond mere service; it fosters a sense of loyalty and trust, as customers feel genuinely heard and appreciated beyond transactional aspects.

Yet, with each advancement, we are faced with critical ethical considerations that demand our focused attention. As AI becomes progressively sophisticated, the challenge of managing privacy in AI-driven communication cannot be overlooked. Visualize hosting a lively party—where everyone is invited to partake, yet privacy must be ensured so that attendees don't inadvertently wander into spaces meant for private conversations. Making sure everyone is covered ethically is another complex challenge. AI systems must be crafted to treat every individual without prejudice or favoritism, embodying the values and principles society cherishes.

Reflection Section: Consider Your Own Experiences

Recall a recent experience involving customer service or a tech-based interaction. How might this interaction have shifted had it included advanced conversational AI? Reflect deeply on any moments of frustration or points where an empathetic, emotionally intelligent response could have changed the course of the interaction positively. Contemplate how this next-generation AI has the potential to transform these past experiences into positive, memorable engagements that leave lasting impressions.

As we look together towards the horizon, the potential of next-generation conversational AI is both thrilling and promising. It offers not only a technological leap forward but also a profound opportunity to build bridges across languages and emotions, forever changing the way we connect and communicate with both machines and each other in this intertwined global tapestry.

AI IN GLOBAL INDUSTRIES: TRANSFORMATIONS ON THE HORIZON

Can you imagine a world where your doctor can predict your health problems before you even get that annoying seasonal flu? Sounds like magic, right? Well, with AI innovations in healthcare, we're inching closer to that reality every day. AI systems are becoming adept at early disease detection, identifying patterns that human eyes might miss. Picture an algorithm that scans medical images with the precision of an eagle eye, flagging anomalies that could signal trouble down the road. Personalized medicine is another fascinating leap. By analyzing your genetic makeup, AI can tailor treatments specifically for you, as if crafting a bespoke suit that fits just right. This approach promises treatments that are not only effective but also minimize side effects, making the journey to health a little less bumpy.

Now, let's wander into the world of finance, where AI is playing the role of a savvy financial advisor. Imagine having an assistant who never sleeps and is always crunching numbers to predict the next big market trend. AI algorithms are doing just that, sifting through mountains of data to spot investment opportunities and assess risks. It's like having a crystal ball guiding your financial decisions with uncanny accuracy. Fraud detection has also entered a new era thanks to AI's vigilance. These systems act like digital watchdogs, sniffing out suspicious transactions faster than you can say "credit card .." They help protect our hard-earned money and maintain trust in financial systems. We will talk more about money and the opportunity you have now and in the future to build a safety nest of passive income with ideas to get rolling with the tools at hand.

In the bustling realm of manufacturing, AI is transforming production lines into symphonies of efficiency. Imagine robots working tirelessly on assembly lines, performing tasks with precision and speed that would put any marathon runner to shame. These automated systems are revolutionizing how products are made, reducing human error and boosting productivity. AI-driven quality control ensures that the products rolling off these lines meet exacting standards, as if inspected by the most meticulous of quality managers. And let's not forget supply chain management. AI optimizes logistics like a seasoned chess player, ensuring materials arrive just in time and in the right quantities. But no worries, we as humans will always be needed to hold the line.

When you think about our vast fields stretching to the horizon, that's where AI is quietly revolutionizing agriculture with a modern twist. Drones equipped with AI soar above these fields, monitoring crop health with the precision of a seasoned farmer. They collect data on everything from soil moisture levels to plant vitality, providing farmers with real-time insights that guide decisions on irrigation and fertilization. Meanwhile, predictive analytics help farmers anticipate weather changes and optimize yield forecasts. It's as if Mother Nature herself has handed over her playbook, allowing farmers to work smarter and more sustainably.

The role of AI in education is nothing short of transformative, offering students personalized learning experiences tailored to their unique needs. Imagine classrooms where AI platforms act as virtual tutors, adapting lessons on the fly based on each student's progress and learning style. These systems offer real-time feedback, helping students grasp complex concepts with ease. For language learners, AI becomes a patient partner, correcting pronunciation and guiding them towards fluency like a gentle coach. Meanwhile, administrative tasks such as enrollment and grading are automated, freeing up educators to focus on what they do best, what they love to do is teach and inspire.

Urban landscapes are also undergoing an AI-driven metamorphosis as cities strive to become more efficient and livable spaces. Intelligent transportation systems are at the forefront, using AI to manage traffic flow and reduce congestion. Imagine a city where autonomous vehicles seamlessly navigate busy streets, communicating with smart traffic lights to ensure smooth transit. Energy management takes another leap forward with smart grids optimizing distribution and minimizing waste. AI even plays a role in community safety, powering surveillance systems that help prevent crime and enhance public security.

In the realm of creativity, AI is an innovative collaborator, transforming how art and music are created. Artists are partnering with algorithms to generate unique digital artworks that push the boundaries of expression. Musicians use AI software to compose original scores or enhance sound mixing, adding a new dimension to their craft. Even writers find inspiration in AI tools that suggest plot twists or assist in editing literary works. These collaborations between human creativity and machine intelligence raise intriguing questions about authorship and originality while opening up exciting new possibilities for artistic exploration.

The future beckons us with endless opportunities where AI seamlessly integrates into our lives and industries just like a trusted partner ready to assist us in enhancing efficiency and creativity alike!

THE ROLE OF AI IN EDUCATION: ENHANCING LEARNING EXPERIENCES

◆ Let’s talk about a classroom brimming with students, no two alike in how they absorb information. Enter AI, a digital maestro, orchestrating personalized learning pathways that cater to each student's unique rhythm. Instead of marching to a one-size-fits-all tune, AI creates customized experiences that adjust in real-time. It's like having a personal tutor who knows exactly when to push harder and when to ease off. These adaptive learning modules analyze how a student interacts with the material and tweak the approach accordingly—think of it as having a teacher who listens not just to what you say but how you say it, adjusting the lesson plan to match your learning style.

And then there are the AI-powered educational tools, the unsung heroes quietly revolutionizing how we teach and learn. Picture a virtual tutor that offers instant feedback on assignments, correcting mistakes before they morph into bad habits. That's the power of AI in play. Language learners benefit too, with AI stepping in as a patient pronunciation coach, deftly guiding them away from "bon-jour" to "bon-JOUR" with the precision of a native speaker. It's an approach that leaves no room for embarrassment or self-doubt, only growth and confidence.

Meanwhile, behind the scenes, AI streamlines administrative tasks with the efficiency of a seasoned conductor leading an orchestra. Student enrollment? Automated. Grading? A breeze. No more late nights for teachers drowning in paperwork; AI handles it all with ease, freeing up educators to focus on what truly matters—nurturing young minds. It's like having an invisible assistant tirelessly working behind the scenes, ensuring that everything runs smoothly without missing a beat.

Yet, while AI's potential is dazzling, it doesn't come without its set of challenges. Consider the digital divide, a chasm that threatens to leave some students in the dust as others sprint ahead. In an ideal world, every student would have access to these AI marvels, but reality paints a different picture. Many schools and communities still struggle with limited resources and outdated technology. Ensuring equitable access is crucial; otherwise, we risk widening the gap between those who have and those who don't.

Integrating AI into education isn't just about weaving technology into the fabric of learning; it's about fostering an environment where every student can thrive. That means providing support and resources to bridge gaps and making sure no one is left behind. The challenge lies in balancing innovation with accessibility, ensuring that AI serves as an equalizer rather than a divider.

Visual Element: Interactive Infographic

Think about creating an interactive infographic showcasing how AI tailors educational experiences at different stages, all ages of early childhood, middle school, high school, and beyond. This visual aid can help you understand the dynamic ways AI adapts to individual learning journeys.

As we move forward, it's clear that AI holds immense promise for enhancing education. But it's more than just deploying advanced algorithms; it's about creating learning experiences that are as diverse as the students themselves. It's about crafting an educational landscape where everyone has the opportunity to flourish, regardless of their starting point. And as we embrace this new era of technology-driven learning, let's remember that at its heart, education is about inspiring curiosity and fostering potential for everyone, not just in those who excel but in every young mind eager to explore the world around them.

SMART CITIES AND AI: BUILDING THE CITIES OF TOMORROW

You know what it feels like to step out of your door into a city that feels alive, almost like it's breathing with you. That's what smart cities are all about using AI to create urban environments that are not just efficient but also sustainable. Picture AI as a kind of urban planner extraordinaire, meticulously designing cities where every element, from streetlights to skyscrapers, is optimized for the best possible experience. Think about traffic flow, for instance. With AI simulations, city planners can predict congestion and design roads that practically guide cars like an invisible force. It’s like having a digital map that changes in real-time, making sure you always take the fastest route, even during rush hour.

Speaking of transportation, how about catching a ride in a city where buses, trains, and even cars seem to glide effortlessly through the streets? This is the magic of intelligent transportation systems powered by AI. These systems work tirelessly to enhance public transportation and reduce traffic jams. Imagine buses that adjust their routes based on real-time data or trains that arrive precisely when you need them. And let's not forget autonomous vehicles—those futuristic rides that navigate urban networks with the precision of a top-tier chauffeur. They promise a future where driving stress is as outdated as dial-up internet.

But there's more to smart cities than just getting from point A to B. Let's talk about energy management and sustainability. Imagine living in a place where energy is distributed so efficiently that waste becomes a thing of the past. Smart grids, powered by AI, are like the conductors of an orchestra, ensuring that every watt of energy is used wisely and nothing goes to waste. And it doesn't stop there. AI plays a crucial role in environmental monitoring too. Imagine a system that efficiently handles waste management by recycling programs that adapt to changing needs, ensuring our cities stay clean and green.

Now, let's shift gears and focus on community engagement and safety, where AI steps in as an unsung hero. Picture AI surveillance systems that act like vigilant guardians, preventing crime before it even happens. These systems can recognize patterns and alert authorities at the first sign of trouble, fostering a sense of security among residents. And when it comes to community connectivity, AI platforms provide channels for citizen feedback and participation. Imagine an app where you can voice concerns about local issues or suggest improvements, knowing that your input is valued and acted upon.

With all these advancements, smart cities are shaping up to be more than just places to live, they're becoming vibrant communities where technology enhances quality of life. It's about creating urban landscapes that are as dynamic as the people who inhabit them, places where innovation meets everyday life in the most seamless way possible. This is the promise of AI in urban planning, a vision of cities that are not only smart but also deeply human-centered.

Soon we will all be able to choose to live in a city where technology isn't just an add-on but an integral part of its fabric, enhancing every aspect from transportation to energy use. It's a vision where cities become smarter by learning from their inhabitants, adapting to their needs, and growing with them over time. Every street corner holds potential for innovation; every park bench offers a chance for relaxation supported by unseen digital threads connecting everything together.

The potential for smart cities is vast, limited only by our imagination and willingness to embrace change. As AI continues its march forward into new frontiers, our urban landscapes will evolve alongside it, becoming more than just spaces we inhabit but environments that inspire us each day anew.

In this era of rapid technological advancement, there's no better time than now to explore what lies ahead for smart cities powered by artificial intelligence. Think of cities where dreams take flight on invisible wings fueled by data-driven insights harnessed for social good. Whether it's reducing carbon footprints through smarter resource allocation or enhancing public safety through predictive analytics, these innovations hold great promise for our future together as urban dwellers seeking harmony between progress and preservation alike.

THE INTERSECTION OF AI AND CREATIVITY: ART, MUSIC, AND MORE

Picture yourself wandering through an art gallery. Each piece of art captivates you, not just because of its beauty, but because it was co-created by an AI. Yes, you heard that right. AI is stepping into the world of visual art, and it's not just dabbling; it's making waves. Algorithms now churn out unique digital artworks, blending colors and themes in ways that often surprise even seasoned artists. Imagine an AI working alongside a painter, suggesting color palettes or brushstroke techniques, pushing the boundaries of what's possible. Artists and AI collaborate like dance partners, each guiding the other to create something neither could achieve alone. It's not about replacing human creativity but enhancing it, opening doors to new artistic expressions that were once unimaginable.

Now, let's shift gears and talk about music. Picture yourself in a recording studio where AI is not just the sound engineer but the composer as well. AI software today can create original compositions that resonate with emotions and complexity. These digital maestros analyze vast libraries of music to understand patterns and styles before composing pieces that feel both novel and familiar. And when it comes to producing music, AI takes on roles like mixing and mastering tracks, ensuring each note hits just right. Musicians are finding new muses in these algorithms, experimenting with melodies and rhythms that defy conventional thinking. It's an exciting time where technology and artistry merge to create sounds that are as innovative as they are harmonious.

The literary world is also embracing AI's creative potential. Picture this: you're staring at a blank page, struggling with writer's block, when an AI tool suggests a plot twist or helps flesh out a character arc. It's like having a brainstorming buddy who's read every book ever written and knows what resonates with readers. These AI tools don't stop at ideation; they assist in editing and proofreading, catching those pesky typos or suggesting more concise phrasing. Writers find themselves liberated from the mechanical aspects of writing, allowing them to focus on storytelling's heart and soul. It's about enhancing the creative process without overshadowing the writer's unique voice.

But with all this innovation come debates that ignite the creative community. One hot topic is copyright and authorship. Who owns the rights to a piece created by an AI? Is it the programmer, the user, or is it shared between them both? It's uncharted territory that challenges our traditional notions of creativity and ownership. Balancing AI's contributions with human expression is another tightrope walk. While AI can mimic styles and techniques, can it truly capture the subtleties of human experience? Or does it merely replicate patterns it's been trained on? These questions stir lively discussions among artists and creators about the role of AI in art.

Textual Element: Case Study on AI Art Collaboration

Consider the collaboration between artist Mario Klingemann and AI in creating "Memories of Passersby I." This installation uses neural networks to generate endless portraits in real-time. It challenges the viewer to consider whether these creations are autonomous art or simply reflections of pre-programmed data.

AI's intersection with creativity is a dynamic landscape filled with possibilities and complexities. As artists explore these new tools, they must navigate the line between innovation and tradition, ensuring technology enhances rather than diminishes the essence of human expression.

PREPARING FOR THE FUTURE: HOW TO STAY AHEAD IN AN AI-DRIVEN WORLD

If we were standing at the edge of a vast ocean, each wave would represent a new technological advancement. In this rapidly evolving seascape, continuous learning and skill development are your life raft. Staying afloat means grabbing onto the ongoing education to keep up with AI's relentless progress. Luckily, there are myriad ways to do this. Think about enrolling in AI courses or certifications that open doors to fresh opportunities. These programs aren't just about acquiring knowledge; they're about fueling your curiosity and expanding your horizons. Workshops and seminars also offer a hands-on approach, giving you a chance to dive into real-world applications alongside fellow learners.

But let's face it, keeping up with tech changes can feel like a never-ending race. The key is to be open to these shifts rather than resist them. Adapting to technological changes involves a mindset shift. It's about seeing digital transformation not as a disruption but as an opportunity to innovate. In the workplace, this might mean adopting new tools that streamline processes or exploring how AI can enhance business strategies. Consider it like updating your wardrobe, or even decluttering, swapping out those old, comfortable jeans for something a bit more modern can make all the difference. Simplify your space and your digital world

Now, let's talk about fostering innovation and creativity in this brave new AI world. Encouraging a culture of innovation isn't just for tech giants; it's crucial for everyone. This involves creating an environment where creative problem-solving is celebrated and interdisciplinary collaboration is the norm. Imagine a room filled with individuals from diverse backgrounds, each bringing unique perspectives to AI projects. This fusion of ideas often sparks breakthroughs that wouldn't happen otherwise. It's kind of like a potluck dinner, where everyone contributes their special dish, resulting in a feast of ideas richer than any individual contribution.

Looking ahead, what future trends should we be ready for? AI's role in shaping future job markets and skill demands is significant. As AI automates routine tasks, there's a growing need for skills that machines can't replicate—think creativity, empathy, and critical thinking. This shift means that staying relevant involves being adaptable and proactive in skill development. It's like preparing for a camping trip; you pack for the unexpected because you know the terrain might change.

As we brave these waters, remember that the goal isn't just to survive but to thrive. By embracing continuous learning, adapting to change, fostering creativity, and anticipating trends, you're not just preparing for the future—you're shaping it. This chapter isn't just an end; it's a beginning, setting the stage for what's next as we delve deeper into how AI continues to reshape our world.

In summary, preparing for an AI-driven future hinges on our willingness to learn and adapt. By staying informed and open to innovation, we equip ourselves with the tools necessary to not only keep pace with change but to steer it in directions that align with our values and aspirations.

As we wrap up this chapter, think of it like packing your bags for a long journey—full of excitement and anticipation for what lies ahead. In the next chapter, we'll explore how AI impacts our personal lives even further, transforming not only how we work but how we live and connect with one another. Stay curious and ready for what's next in this thrilling adventure!

9
MAKE MONEY REMOTELY USING CHATGPT🧠

IMAGINE WAKING up to the gentle rustle of leaves outside your window, the sun casting a warm glow across your workspace. Your office isn't confined to four walls; it's wherever you choose to be. This is the essence of running a business remotely, a lifestyle that blends work with the freedom to explore, create, and live on your own terms, anywhere you want.

In today's digital age, the traditional boundaries of the workplace have dissolved. With a laptop and a reliable internet connection, you can manage projects, communicate with clients, and oversee operations from virtually anywhere. This shift isn't just about location; it's about embracing a mindset that values flexibility, autonomy, and innovation.

Starting a remote business begins with identifying your strengths and passions. Whether it's consulting, digital marketing, e-commerce, or content creation, the opportunities are vast. The key is to leverage your skills to offer value to a global audience. With tools like ChatGPT, you can brainstorm ideas, draft proposals, and even automate customer interactions, streamlining your workflow and enhancing productivity.

Communication is the lifeblood of any business, and in a remote setting, it's paramount. Utilizing platforms like Zoom, Slack, or Microsoft Teams ensures that you're always connected with your team and clients. Regular check-ins, clear expectations, and transparent processes foster trust and collaboration, bridging the physical gap between team members.

Time management becomes both a challenge and an opportunity in remote work. Without the structure of a traditional office, it's essential to establish routines that balance work and personal life. Setting specific work hours, taking regular breaks, and creating a dedicated workspace can enhance focus and prevent burnout.Traqq | traqq.com+1Wikipedia+1Barron's+1People.com+1

Financial management is another critical aspect. With various digital tools available, tracking expenses, invoicing clients, and managing budgets have become more accessible. Platforms like QuickBooks or FreshBooks offer user-friendly interfaces to keep your finances in check, ensuring your business remains profitable and sustainable.

Marketing your services or products requires a strategic approach. Social media platforms, content marketing, and SEO are powerful tools to reach your target audience. Engaging content, consistent branding, and authentic storytelling can set you apart in a crowded digital marketplace.

Continuous learning and adaptability are the cornerstones of a successful remote business. The digital landscape is ever-evolving, and staying updated with the latest trends, tools, and best practices ensures you remain competitive. Investing time in online courses, webinars, and networking can open doors to new opportunities and collaborations.

Ultimately, running a business from anywhere is about more than just work; it's about crafting a lifestyle that aligns with your values and aspirations. It's about waking up each day with purpose, knowing that you're in control of your journey. Embrace the freedom, the challenges, and the endless possibilities that come with remote entrepreneurship. Your adventure awaits.

Turn AI Into Your Digital Sidekick for Income From Anywhere

You don't need a business degree, tech background, or a big following to make money online anymore. With ChatGPT, your ideas, services, and digital products can take shape faster than ever, often with zero startup cost.

This chapter will walk you through practical ways to earn income remotely using ChatGPT, how to use it to save time and boost output, and where to start even if you feel overwhelmed by tech.

📌 Why ChatGPT Is a Game Changer for Earning Online

ChatGPT can speed up or fully support many remote income activities:

Writing (articles, emails, resumes)

Editing and polishing (grammatical corrections, tone adjustments)

Idea generation (business ideas, course outlines, social media hooks)

Automation (scripting for emails, task breakdowns, customer responses)

Product creation (eBooks, prompt packs, lead magnets)

Niche	How ChatGPT Helps	Where to Sell
Freelance writing	Generate blog posts, articles, ad copy	Fiverr, Upwork, Medium
eBook publishing	Structure, write, and edit full-length books	Amazon KDP, Gumroad
Social media services	Create content calendars and captions	Instagram, LinkedIn, Facebook
Resume/cover letter help	Improve clarity, grammar, tone	LinkedIn, Indeed, direct sales
Digital templates	Design planners, checklists, or worksheets	Etsy, Payhip, Notion
Prompt engineering	Build and sell prompt collections	Gumroad, PromptBase
Online courses	Outline and script course content	Teachable, Thinkific

These abilities empower you to step confidently into the gig economy, digital product market, or remote freelance world—even if you're just starting.

📌 Reference:

OpenAI's ChatGPT Capabilities Overview explains its broad applications across content generation, planning, and business support. [OpenAI, 2024]

◆ Step 1: Identify a Service or Product You Can Offer

Here are some beginner-friendly remote income paths that ChatGPT can support:

🛠 Prompt Example:

"Write a 600-word blog post on 'Time-Saving Tips for Remote Workers.' Include three actionable tips, a friendly tone, and an SEO headline."

◆ Step 2: Use ChatGPT to Build the Product or Service

For eBooks or Guides:

Prompt: "Outline a short eBook titled 'Beginner's Guide to Starting an Online Side Hustle.' Include chapters and subpoints."

For Templates or Printables:

Prompt: "Create a weekly productivity planner for remote freelancers. Include categories for tasks, deadlines, and motivational quotes."

For Gigs or Services:

Prompt: "Write a professional Fiverr gig description for someone offering custom email writing services with AI assistance."

◆ Step 3: Set Up Your Platform

Once you've created your offer, choose a platform to launch:

Platform	What It's Good For
Fiverr/Upwork	Service-based work like resumes, blog posts
Etsy	Selling digital templates and planners
Amazon KDP	Publishing eBooks or journals
Gumroad	Selling prompt packs, courses, downloads
Substack	Monetized newsletters
Teachable	Hosting online courses

📌 Reference:

Gumroad's beginner guide outlines how digital creators can launch with zero upfront cost. [Gumroad, 2024]

🔹 Step 4: Market It with AI Support

Marketing doesn't have to be overwhelming. ChatGPT can write for you:

Emails

"Write a welcome email for people who downloaded my free remote work checklist."

Social media posts

"Create 3 Instagram captions to promote a new eBook on time management."

SEO optimization

“Give me 10 high-traffic keywords for ‘remote income for beginners’.”

Sales page copy

“Write a persuasive sales description for a digital productivity planner.”

📌 Reference:

Capterra’s digital marketing guide shows how AI tools boost solo-preneur visibility online. [Capterra, 2024]

🔹 Step 5: Stay Consistent with an AI Productivity Plan

Even small daily actions add up. Use ChatGPT to plan and automate your goals.

Prompt:

“Create a 30-day checklist for building my freelance writing profile online, including daily LinkedIn actions and writing goals.”

Prompt:

“Give me a weekly content plan for promoting my Etsy printable store.”

⭐ Pro Tips to Maximize Your Earning Potential

Start small: Your first $10 online proves it's possible. Then scale.

Test multiple prompts: Slight changes can improve output dramatically.

Collect testimonials: Ask ChatGPT to help you draft client feedback forms.

Automate repetitive tasks: Use AI to handle FAQs, scheduling, and editing.

Final Thought

You don't need to wait for permission, credentials, or a fancy title to start earning. With curiosity, persistence, and ChatGPT as your assistant, you can build an income stream on your terms—from anywhere with Wi-Fi.

Let this chapter be your launchpad. The only thing left to do is start.

CONCLUSION

Well, here we are at the end of our journey together. Imagine us sitting in a cozy café, steaming mugs in hand, as we reflect on the path we've traveled. We've covered a lot of ground, haven't we? From the mysterious realms of AI to the practicalities of prompt engineering, it's been quite the adventure. But you did it! You took that initial tech fear by the horns and wrestled it into submission. So, let's take a moment to celebrate that.

Throughout this book, we've explored what AI really is—no, not the kind that dreams of world domination, but the kind that makes life a tad easier. We dove into prompt engineering, which is a fancy way of saying we learned how to talk to machines more effectively. We also ventured into ways AI can sneak into your daily routine and make everything from sending emails to managing your calendar less of a chore. And we didn't just stop there. We tackled the big kahuna: using ChatGPT to unlock remote income opportunities. Imagine working from a hammock on a beach somewhere—now that's living the dream!

Now, as you close this chapter, take a moment to pat yourself on the back. You started this book with questions, perhaps a little trepidation, and now look at you! You're ready to embrace AI like an old friend. You've gained insights into how machines learn, how to craft the perfect prompt, and how to integrate this knowledge into your everyday life. You're practically an AI whisperer!

But let's not pretend the journey is over. There are still uncharted waters out there—AI is a vast and ever-changing field. Perhaps you're still wondering how to apply all this knowledge or facing new challenges as you experiment with AI tools. That's perfectly okay. The key is to keep learning, keep exploring, and most importantly, keep having fun with it. Think of it as a never-ending story where you're both the protagonist and the author.

So, what's next? Use these newfound skills in real-world scenarios. Whether it's enhancing your productivity, launching a side hustle, or simply impressing your friends at dinner parties with your AI lingo, put what you've learned into action. Let AI be your co-pilot as you navigate both personal and professional landscapes. The possibilities are as endless as they are exciting.

As you continue this journey, remember that learning is a lifelong adventure. Stay curious and keep your finger on the pulse of technological advancements. Sign up for online courses, join AI communities, and dive into books that further pique your interest. The world of AI is like an onion or a parfait, delicious layered and rich. There is much to discover that is yet to be uncovered.

I've listed some resources at the end of this book to help guide your continued exploration. Consider them your treasure map to AI's hidden gems. And, of course, I want to extend a heartfelt thank you for letting me be part of your journey. It's been an absolute pleasure to share this adventure with you.

If you ever feel like reaching out to share your AI successes, struggles, or just a funny story about how ChatGPT saved your bacon, please do. We're all in this together, and your experiences can inspire others on their path.

As you step forward, remember this: AI is not just a tool, but a gateway to new possibilities for yourself and your family.for generations to come until Jesus returns. . Approach it with excitement and an open mind while creating streams of income on line. Who knows what amazing opportunities await you? You're not just embracing AI; you're embracing a future filled with potential. So go ahead, explore, innovate, and let your imagination with prayer be your compass. The world is waiting, and it's yours to discover.

Now you have everything you need to create streams of income online, master AI prompts, boost productivity, and generate wealth from anywhere—

it's time to pass on your newfound knowledge and show other readers where they can find the same help.

Simply by leaving your honest opinion of this book on Amazon, you'll show other **curious beginners and aspiring remote workers** where they can find the information they're looking for, and pass their passion for **simplifying tech and unlocking digital potential** forward.

Thank you for your help. The learning is kept alive when we pass on our knowledge—and you're helping **me** do just that.

Click here to leave your review on Amazon.

REFERENCES

- *ChatGPT Capabilities Overview* https://help.openai.com/en/articles/9260256-chatgpt-capabilities-overview
- *Debunking the Myths of Artificial Intelligence* https://pmc.ncbi.nlm.nih.gov/articles/PMC6266534/
- *Artificial Intelligence and Automation: Decoding Human ...* https://www.eit.edu.au/artificial-intelligence-decoding-human-fears/
- *The impact of (rapid) technology adoption on employee ...* https://www.sciencedirect.com/science/article/pii/S0040162522003845
- *Curb Your Tech Stress with Mindfulness Techniques* https://www.itssimplyplaced.com/wellness-wednesday-curb-your-tech-stress-with-mindfulness-techniques/
- *Overcoming the Fear of Technology as a Young Woman* https://www.linkedin.com/pulse/overcoming-fear-technology-young-woman-refactoryug-ombqf
- *A Beginner's Guide to Engineering Prompts in ChatGPT ...* https://medium.com/@matthew.edgar.ritchie/a-beginners-guide-to-engineering-prompts-in-chatgpt-and-other-ai-tools-f8dbec88a309
- *Overcoming AI Fears: A Beginner's Guide* https://www.learningtree.com/blog/overcoming-ai-fears-beginners-guide/
- *The ultimate guide to writing effective AI prompts* https://www.atlassian.com/blog/artificial-intelligence/ultimate-guide-writing-ai-prompts
- *8 of the Best AI Productivity Tools to Help You Optimize ...* https://buffer.com/resources/ai-productivity-tools/
- *What is AI Automation? All You Need to Know* https://www.blueprism.com/guides/ai-automation/
- *AI and the Future of Remote Work | Edvisors* https://www.edvisors.com/blog/ai-and-remote-work/#:~:text=AI%20is%20set%20to%20profoundly,new%20roles%2C%20and%20fostering%20innovation.
- *The 10 Best AI Tools for Time Management* https://slack.com/blog/productivity/the-10-best-ai-tools-for-time-management
- *How Freelance Writers Can Master ChatGPT for Content ...* https://medium.com/@rayzielrafael/how-freelance-writers-can-master-chatgpt-for-content-creation-the-ultimate-100-word-guide-9ba49666edc8
- *AI Tools For Consulting* https://www.ibm.com/think/topics/ai-tools-for-consulting

- *Ecommerce AI: Transforming How Companies Do Business* https://www.bigcommerce.com/articles/ecommerce/ecommerce-ai/
- *Tools for AI Market Research: Turn Data Into Insights* https://www.qualtrics.com/experience-management/research/ai-market-research/
- *The privacy paradox with AI* https://www.reuters.com/legal/legalindustry/privacy-paradox-with-ai-2023-10-31/
- *AI Data Security: Complete Guide & Best Practices* https://bigid.com/blog/ai-data-security/
- *Bridging Technology and Empathy: AI in Human-Centered ...* https://anthro-tech.com/ideas-and-insights/ai-impact-on-hcd
- *Biased Technology: The Automated Discrimination of Facial ...* https://www.aclu-mn.org/en/news/biased-technology-automated-discrimination-facial-recognition#:~:text=Studies%20show%20that%20facial%20recognition,Facial%20recognition%20automates%20discrimination.
- *10 Must-Read AI Books | Data Literacy* https://dataliteracy.com/10-must-read-ai-books/
- *AI for Everyone* https://www.coursera.org/learn/ai-for-everyone
- *AI News | Latest AI News, Analysis & Events* https://www.artificialintelligence-news.com/
- *The future of conversational AI: key trends to watch* https://boost.ai/blog/conversational-ai-future/
- *AI Will Transform the Global Economy. Let's Make Sure It ...* https://www.imf.org/en/Blogs/Articles/2024/01/14/ai-will-transform-the-global-economy-lets-make-sure-it-benefits-humanity
- *Artificial Intelligence in Education 2023: A Year in Review* https://ciddl.org/artificial-intelligence-in-education-2023-a-year-in-review/#:~:text=One%20of%20the%20standout%20trends,educational%20content%20to%20individual%20needs.
- *Artificial Intelligence in the Smart City — A Literature Review* https://www.researchgate.net/publication/376970158_Artificial_Intelligence_in_the_Smart_City_-_A_Literature_Review

BONUS PROMPTS LIST TO GET YOU STARTED

🛒 **E-Commerce & Product Sales**

1. "List 10 profitable digital products I can create and sell online."
2. "Help me brainstorm a unique Etsy product using recycled materials."
3. "Write an Amazon product description for a yoga mat targeting seniors."
4. "What trending products can I dropship in 2025?"
5. "Create a Shopify homepage layout that builds trust and boosts conversions."
6. "How can I turn my hobby of making candles into an online store?"
7. "Give me SEO keywords for selling handmade dog accessories."
8. "Write a product launch email for a new eco-friendly water bottle."
9. "Generate a monthly content plan for my online soap business."

10. "Create an Instagram caption that promotes my online mug shop."

Freelance Writing & Content Creation

1. "List 20 blog topics in the wellness niche that pay well."
2. "Rewrite this article in a more conversational tone for a U.S. audience."
3. "Create an outline for a 1,200-word blog post on AI in education."
4. "What types of companies hire freelance writers on retainer?"
5. "Generate 5 cold email templates for pitching blog writing services."
6. "Turn this LinkedIn post into a Medium article."
7. "Help me create a Fiverr gig for editing non-fiction eBooks."
8. "Make a list of platforms that pay for original stories or poems."
9. "What are high-demand writing niches in 2025?"
10. "Generate a content calendar for a freelance travel writer."

Online Courses & Coaching

1. "Create a course outline to teach beginner watercolor painting."
2. "Write a sales page for my productivity coaching program."
3. "What software do I need to create and sell my first mini-course?"
4. "Give me 10 names for an online parenting workshop."
5. "How can I use Zoom to host a weekly wellness coaching group?"
6. "Write a script for a 5-minute course intro video on passive income."

7. “What should I include in a 4-week self-confidence challenge?”
8. “Turn my life coaching method into a 7-module online course.”
9. “Create a landing page layout to attract coaching clients.”
10. “Write an upsell offer for my digital course.”

💻 Tech & Digital Services

1. “List 10 digital services I can offer if I’m good at Canva.”
2. “Create a pitch for managing small business social media accounts.”
3. “Help me price my podcast editing services for new clients.”
4. “Write an onboarding email for a new web design client.”
5. “Generate a step-by-step SEO audit checklist.”
6. “Make a tagline for my virtual assistant business.”
7. “Create a gig description for a Squarespace website designer.”
8. “How can I offer Notion template setups for productivity?”
9. “What remote tech jobs require no coding?”
10. “Build a simple proposal for WordPress site management.”

📱 Social Media & Influencer Income

1. “What are the top niches to build a profitable Instagram page in 2025?”
2. “Write a YouTube video script on the ‘digital nomad lifestyle.’”
3. “How can I use Pinterest to drive traffic to my affiliate blog?”
4. “Create a list of brand sponsors who pay micro-influencers.”
5. “Generate 10 TikTok hooks for a side hustle content channel.”

6. "How can I monetize a small YouTube channel with under 1,000 subs?"
7. "Make a weekly social media plan for a beginner influencer."
8. "What affiliate programs pay the highest commissions in 2025?"
9. "Draft an email pitch to a brand for Instagram sponsorship."
10. "Outline 5 Instagram reel ideas to promote a digital planner."

📖 Self-Publishing & Printables

1. "What are bestselling low-content books I can create in 2025?"
2. "Create 10 prompts for a self-reflection journal I'm publishing."
3. "List 5 profitable niches for printable planners on Etsy."
4. "Write a title and subtitle for a gratitude journal for men."
5. "How can I use KDP to publish a children's coloring book?"
6. "Give me a keyword list for selling habit trackers online."
7. "Write an Amazon description for a digital detox workbook."
8. "Design a promotional email for a printable meal planner bundle."
9. "Outline a simple devotional for busy moms I can sell on Gumroad."
10. "Turn this checklist into a printable productivity worksheet."

📊 Consulting & Expertise-Based Services

1. "What services can I offer online as a retired teacher?"
2. "Write a profile summary for a freelance HR consultant."

3. “How can I use my accounting background to offer remote services?”
4. “List 10 remote business ideas for therapists or counselors.”
5. “Draft a LinkedIn summary for a virtual marketing strategist.”
6. “Write a short bio for a resume review consultant.”
7. “Create an FAQ page for an online parenting coach.”
8. “How can I market myself as a digital declutter expert?”
9. “What kind of consulting services are popular post-2024?”
10. “Help me write my first client welcome packet.”

Creative & Artistic Income Streams

1. “How do I sell my photography as digital downloads?”
2. “Generate a list of art niches that sell well on Redbubble.”
3. “Write an artist bio for my online print shop.”
4. “What are the best sites to sell AI-generated art?”
5. “Help me market my black-and-white illustrations for books.”
6. “Create a product description for a custom pet portrait.”
7. “What creative passive income streams work for crafters?”
8. “How can I turn my calligraphy into an online business?”
9. “Design a tagline for a personalized art business.”
10. “List 5 art challenge themes to build a following on Instagram.”

Knowledge Sharing & Microtasks

1. “List 10 places I can get paid to answer questions online.”
2. “Write a compelling profile for Upwork tutoring jobs.”
3. “How do I start offering paid advice calls via Zoom?”
4. “Generate a welcome message for my tutoring clients.”
5. “What microtask platforms are legit in 2025?”
6. “Create a professional gig title for a proofreading job.”

7. “How do I build a niche audience on Quora for affiliate links?”
8. “Help me build a paid group Q&A community.”
9. “Create a marketing blurb for a remote math tutor.”
10. “List knowledge-based services I can offer with only a smartphone.”

💰 Passive Income & Automation

1. “What are 5 passive income models I can build with ChatGPT?”
2. “Create an outline for an evergreen email sales funnel.”
3. “How do I automate affiliate marketing with AI tools?”
4. “Generate a year-long content schedule for passive income ideas.”
5. “What digital products can I sell on autopilot through Etsy?”
6. “Write a 7-day email series to promote a course while I sleep.”
7. “What are the pros and cons of monetizing a blog vs YouTube?”
8. “Turn my webinar script into an automated course funnel.”
9. “What are the best tools for passive income with no audience?”
10. “Generate a productivity system to manage multiple income streams.”

Side Hustles & Smart Niches

1. “How can I use ChatGPT to build a resume writing side hustle?”
2. “List 10 flexible side hustles for stay-at-home parents.”
3. “Create a 30-day challenge to build my first $1k online.”

4. "Give me niche ideas for a subscription box I can run from home."
5. "Help me market a proofreading side hustle to ESL students."
6. "How can I make money remotely if I only have 1 hour per day?"
7. "Create a checklist for starting a no-code online business."
8. "List 5 overlooked side hustles that require no upfront cost."
9. "Help me build a side hustle around my love for organizing."
10. "How can I test my remote business idea with no website?"

www.ingramcontent.com/pod-product-compliance
Lightning Source LLC
LaVergne TN
LVHW022224200926
848481LV00006B/2114